Kaleidoscope

1 Reading and Writing

Anita Sökmen
University of Washington

Daphne Mackey
University of Washington

HOUGHTON MIFFLIN COMPANY   Boston   New York

Sponsoring Editor: Susan Maguire
Senior Associate Editor: Kathleen Sands Boehmer
Associate Project Editor: Gabrielle Stone
Senior Production/Design Coordinator: Carol Merrigan
Senior Manufacturing Coordinator: Marie Barnes
Marketing Manager: Elaine Leary
Cover Design: Ha Nguyen
Cover Image: Hot Air Ballooning, © Miyazaki Yoichiro-FPG International.

Page 44: Courtesy of Grand Wailea Resort, Hotel & Spa.
Page 45: Courtesy of Abigail's Hotel.
Page 45: Courtesy of Bali Intercontinental Resort.
Page 48: Based on Roylance, Frank D., "Space Travel: A vacation on the moon . . . one great step for tourism, from the *Baltimore Sun,* reprinted in *The Seattle Times,* Sunday, October 20, 1996 (p. K12).
Page 93: Adapted from "Frequently Asked Questions About Tenants' Rights" by Assemblyman Richard Gottfried, as published on TenantNet at http://www.tenant.net/Rights/gottf.txt. Used by permission.
Pages 121–122: Adapted from Barbara Combs, "Reach Out and Touch Someone— Electronically," *The Seattle Times*, Sunday, March 30, 1997. Used by permission of The Seattle Times.
Page 130: Based on "E-mail Snooping Is OK in the Eyes of the Law" from *Wall Street Journal*, March 19, 1996, p. A1.
Page 180: Reprinted with the permission of Margaret K. McElderry Books, an imprint of Simon & Schuster Children's Publishing Division, from *A Suitcase Full of Seaweed* by Janet S. Wong. Copyright © 1996 by Janet S. Wong.
Page 186: Adapted with permission from "Here's Why Wives Complain" by Tracy L. Pipp, *Detroit News*, as printed in *The Seattle Times*, Monday, March 24, 1997, p. E2.

www.hmco.com/college

Printed in the U.S.A.

Library of Congress Catalog Card Number: 97-72516

ISBN: 0-395-85880-1

1 2 3 4 5 6 7 8 9–QF–02 01 00 99 98

To Anita's father, Robert J. Kain, and to Daphne's parents, Daphne and George Mackey.

Acknowledgments
We would like to thank our families for their support and understanding as we turned our focus to our computers. We are grateful for the feedback of colleagues and students at the University of Washington. In particular, we thank Cara Izumi, Eleanor Holstein, Lesley Lin, Jane Power, Jim Ward and Nancy Ackles, for her knowledge of article use. We also appreciated the comments of reviewers: Victoria Badalamenti, LaGuardia Community College; Brenda Bayeur, ELS Language Centers; Anne Berry, Georgetown University; Gretchen Bitterlin, San Diego Community College; Joseph Chapple, EF International School; Marjorie Friedman, ELS Language Center; Jane George, Boston University; Janet Goldstein, Bramson ORT Technical Institute; Virginia Heringer, Pasadena City College; Grazyna Boguta Kenda, The College for Technology; Grace Low, University of Oregon; Dennis Oliver, Arizona State University; June Orhnberger, Suffolk Community College; Jeanne Perrin, Title IV Director; Meridith Pike-Baky, University of California at Berkeley; Kathy Sherak, San Francisco State University; Steve Shin, ELS Language Centers; Adrianne Sklar, Concordia University; Rafaela Volpe, Norwalk Community Technical College; and Donna Warren, Edmonds Community College. Thanks also to the people at Houghton Mifflin: Susan Maguire, who brought us on board; Kathy Smith, who kept us on track; and Lauren Wilson, who kept track of everything.

Contents

Unit 2   Where in the World?   *29*

4 Adventure Travel   *30*

5 Decisions, Decisions   *36*

6 Wish You Were Here   *47*

Unit 4   The E-mail Revolution   *100*

Preface

Kaleidoscope 1: Reading and Writing provides high-beginning students with a variety of tasks designed to improve reading and writing skills. It is based on the premises that students

- need more than humanities-based types of writing experiences.
- need to develop a working vocabulary for a variety of topics.
- need to learn how to edit their own work.

Overview

Kaleidoscope 1 introduces students to the fundamentals of academic, business, and practical everyday writing. Specifically, the text

- integrates reading and writing skills.
- focuses on vocabulary development, a key skill in both reading and writing.
- works on key reading skills that help prepare students to deal with authentic texts.
- focuses on multigenre writing.
- includes **Preparing to Write** and **Editing and Rewriting** criteria that help less-experienced instructors feel comfortable with different types of writing assignments.
- uses task-based exercises as much as possible to keep students involved and to reduce wordiness in the text.
- allows each student to stay within his or her comfort level for sharing information and experiences.
- includes ideas for class activities.
- includes a **Reference** section with such helpful information as spelling rules, irregular verb forms, rules for using and forming comparatives and superlatives, and formats for formal business letters.

Features

With some variation, the chapters include these main elements and follow this general format:

Starting Point   Connects students to the topic of the chapter.

Reading	Includes reading selections and exercises that focus on comprehension, skill building, and vocabulary skills.
Targeting	Helps students work with vocabulary and key expressions related to a topic or a type of writing.
Writing	Includes **Preparing to Write** activities that help students develop ideas and write in a variety of formats. The length of compositions has been left open to fit the curricula of various programs.
Editing and Rewriting	Teaches students how to edit their own writing, with a focus on the most common mistakes in writing and suggestions for what students ought to look for as they check their work. The **Editing Checklist** includes questions for students to use in editing their peers' writing and their own writing.

Additional activities in *Kaleidoscope 1* include **Quickwriting** and suggestions for a **Class Activity** to round out many of the topics. Depending on whether the writing and editing activities are done during class, each chapter will take from one to three hours of class time. Exercises that have answers in the back of the book are marked with the (ANSWER KEY) icon.

Because becoming self-editors is an overwhelming task for ESL students, we suggest training students to do multiple passes through their compositions, focusing on one type of error at a time. They will have a better chance of finding errors this way than if they are trying to find all types of mistakes. For this reason, editing exercises focus on one type of error at a time. As each type has been practiced in class, encourage students to build up a routine of multiple passes through their work in the editing stage. For example,

- one pass through to look for sentence completeness
- one pass to focus on verb tenses
- another pass to look at nouns: do they need an article? do they need to be plural?

As the term progresses, your feedback on writing will help students know what type of error they should pay most attention to.

Student Notebook

We suggest that students use a reading/writing notebook. Possible uses for the notebook include

- quickwriting, as indicated in the text.
- journal writing, if teachers find this activity beneficial.
- keeping track of outside reading with a reading "log" and brief notes about readings, such as new vocabulary, questions, and interesting ideas.
- reflecting on their progress as writers—what they have learned after completing their work on a topic.

Vocabulary Strategies

In order for students to learn the new vocabulary that they record in their notebooks, they need to use it. Here are some suggestions for additional activities that will help students practice the vocabulary.

- Have students look in newspapers or magazines for vocabulary that they have studied in *Kaleidoscope 1*. Have them write down the sentences they find and share them with the class.
- Have students find words in their notebooks from different chapters that could be used in a conversation. Have them write that conversation.
- Ask them to find five adjectives from their notebooks and, working in small groups, to determine the opposites. Have them make a matching exercise to give to other groups.
- Suggest that students look through the vocabulary in their notebooks for words that are related in meaning. They can then make up related-word lists with one word that doesn't fit. Have them write sentences or paragraphs using some of the related words.
- Ask students to choose *phrasal verbs* (verbs with prepositions) or *collocations* (groups of words that go together) from the vocabulary in their notebooks. Have them write sentences with these expressions, leaving a blank line for one of the words in the expression. They can then take turns quizzing the other students on the missing words.
- Have students make flash cards by writing words and short definitions on opposite sides of index cards to practice with or use in a game.
- Create a vocabulary search game by giving students a certain amount of time to find words in their notebooks related to work, exercise, family, and other topics.

- Have students list nouns from their notebooks and use dictionaries to find the other forms in that word family. Students can teach these forms to the class.
- Ask students to find words that have the same suffix, prefix, or root. Have them compile the results in a chart.
- Have students make drawings to represent words from their notebooks and have their classmates guess the words.
- Have students work in groups to make a crossword puzzle of words from their notebooks. Then, they can exchange their puzzles with classmates.
- In a game of word clues, have students choose words from their notebooks and write them on slips of paper. Working in pairs, each student chooses a word and gives clues about it to his or her partner, who tries to guess the word. After five minutes, have them change roles or switch partners.
- In group brainstorming, have students think of synonyms for words from their notebooks. They may use a dictionary. Make a scrambled list of the synonyms and use them for a matching quiz. Do the same for antonyms.
- Have students choose five words from their notebooks and survey native speakers for the first word that comes to mind when they hear the target word. Ask them to share the word association results with the rest of the class.

KALEIDOSCOPE 1 AT A GLANCE*

Unit	Reading	Preparing to Write	Writing	Targeting Language	Editing & Rewriting
1 First Things First	• scanning (1) • skimming (2) • analyzing information (3)	• from sentence to paragraph (1) • ways to describe yourself (2) • introductory sentences (3)	• paragraph (1, 3) • description of self (2) • paragraph with an introductory sentence	• countries, languages, nationalities (1) • adjectives & nouns (2) • collocations (3)	• sentence punctuation & capitalization (2)
2 Where in the World?	• taking notes (4) • reading charts (5) • identifying problems (5) • analyzing information (6)	• writing requests (5) • address format (6) • organizing information (7)	• fax to request information (5) • postcard (6) • travel brochure (7)	• adjectives to describe places (4) • nouns & verbs (5) • adjectives to describe an experience (6)	• present & present progressive (6) • matching writing & audience (7)
3 Living Spaces	• finding specific information (8) • taking notes in a chart (9) • comparing ideas/analyzing organization (10) • making inferences (11)	• picturing the details (8) • conducting a survey/planning a chart (9) • including details (11)	• description of a room (8) • survey results in a chart (9) • letter of complaint (11)	• spatial prepositions (8) • word forms (11)	• subject/verb agreement (includes commas in a series) (8)

*The numbers in parentheses refer to chapters.

1 First Things First

When you first meet people or when you first move to a new place, what do you do? Usually, you have to take care of a lot of questions and details. In this unit you will focus on some typical first situations and tasks.

These are some of the activities you will do in this unit:

- Learn about your classmates
- Read information in forms
- Complete forms
- Read descriptions of people
- Write a formal letter
- Write a description of yourself
- Write about a changed living situation

Chapter 1

Who's Who?

Forms and applications are part of everyday life. You will often fill them out. This chapter gives you practice in reading and completing forms with information about yourself and other people.

Starting Point

Getting to Know a Classmate and Completing Forms

Choose a classmate and complete this form with information from that person. If necessary, look at the questions after the form to help you.

Name: _____ _____
 (first/given) *(last/family)*

Nationality: _____ First language: _____
 (country)

Age: _____ Single or Married: _____
 (marital status)

Living: ❑ with a family ❑ alone ❑ with a roommate

Living in: ❑ an apartment ❑ a house ❑ a dormitory

In: _____
 (city or town)

Favorite free-time activity: _____

_____

What _____ your name?

Where are you _____?

_____ do you live?

How old _____ you?

Are you single or _____?

What _____ your native language?

Do you live in a house or apartment?

What is your favorite free-time activity?

Reading

Student Information Cards

All these students want to live in English House. You are on the Housing Committee, and you help decide where they will live.

1. **Scan** the information on the cards below. How are the students similar? How are they different? Which students would be good roommates?

READING TIP

When you read, you don't always need to read every word. When you **scan** something, you look only for specific information.

Name: Mayumi Nakata   From: Japan

Language: Japanese

Age: 18   M/F: F   Smoker: ☐ Y ☑ N

Favorite free-time activities: going to movies, shopping

Name: Walter Schmidt   From: Germany

Language: German

Age: 21   M/F: M   Smoker: ☐ Y ☑ N

Favorite free-time activities: using the computer, playing tennis

Name: Marta Diaz   From: Mexico
Language: Spanish

Age: 21   M/F: F   Smoker: ☐ Y ☑ N

Favorite free-time activities: running, using the computer

Name: Byong Kim   From: South Korea
Language: Korean

Age: 23   M/F: M   Smoker: ☑ Y ☐ N

Favorite free-time activities: going to movies, playing a guitar

Name: Carlos Sandoval   From: Colombia
Language: Spanish

Age: 22   M/F: M   Smoker: ☐ Y ☑ N

Favorite free-time activities: playing tennis, bicycling

Name: Hiromi Nakai   From: Japan
Language: Japanese

Age: 19   M/F: F   Smoker: ☑ Y ☐ N

Favorite free-time activities: listening to music, going to movies

Name: Danielle Le Duc   From: Canada
Language: French and English

Age: 18   M/F: F   Smoker: ☐ Y ☑ N

Favorite free-time activities: hiking, swimming

Name: Jamal Al-Aziz   From: Kuwait
Language: Arabic

Age: 20   M/F: M   Smoker: ☑ Y ☐ N

Favorite free-time activities: listening to music, spending time with friends

2. *Match the best roommates and write their names on rooms in this illustration. Put two students in each room.*

Mayumi Nakata
and

3. *Some students would be good roommates and some would not. Why? Complete the following sentences with your ideas. Then share your ideas with a classmate. The first one is an example.*

Mayumi Nakata and Byong Kim are alike because they both like
name of student / name of student

to go to the movies.

_____ and _____ are not alike because _____
name of student / name of student / name of student

likes to _____ and _____ likes to _____.
name of student

_____ and _____ both like to _____.
name of student / name of student

_____ and _____ would not have a problem because
name of student / name of student

_____.

Targeting

Country, Language, and Nationality Words

When you fill out forms, you need to know the words for countries, languages, and nationalities.

1. *Study these rules. Country, language, and nationality words are always capitalized.*

Rules	Examples
The name of a country	Liu is from **China.** Anna is from **Spain.**
The name of a language	He speaks **Chinese.** She speaks **Spanish.**
The nationality	He is **Chinese.** She is **Spanish.**

2. *Complete this chart with the correct words. Use the information on the student cards on pages 4–5. Add other countries of people in your class. The first one has been done for you.*

Country	Nationality	Language
China	Chinese	Chinese Cantonese Mandarin
Mexico		
		Spanish
	Kuwaiti	

Country	Nationality	Language
Canada		
	Korean	
		German
	Japanese	
(your country)		
(other country)		

3. Complete the sentences with the correct words. Use the country, language, and nationality words in this chapter. The first one has been done for you.

ANSWER KEY

a.   Last year I visited <u> Kuwait </u> and Saudi Arabia on my trip
                                 (1)

to the Middle East. I studied _____ before I went so that I
                                       (2)

would be able to understand people. On the way back, I

stopped in Paris. I didn't get many opportunities to speak

_____ because so many people spoke English. I'm sorry
      (3)

that I didn't have a chance to visit any cities in _____,
                                              (4)

such as Berlin.

b.   We have students from a lot of different places in my

class. One of my South American classmates is from

_____. The three _____ students are all from Tokyo.

(5)   (6)

One of them visited Thailand last year. She changed planes

at the airport in Seoul. It was a short stopover, so she didn't

get to visit any places in _____.

(7)

c.   My _____ grandmother always called me Juan

(8)

instead of John. _____ borders the United States.

(9)

d.   More people speak _____ than any other language

(10)

in the world.

4. *Correct the country, nationality, and language name mistakes in these sentences.*

                                                French

a.   Everything in Canada is written in English and ~~France~~.

b.   People speak Portuguese in Portugal and Brazilian.

c.   One of my classmates is from Colombian.

d.   There are three Japan students in my class.

e.   Have you ever eaten India food?

f.   We went to a Greece restaurant.

g.   Mexico is in North American.

h.   In Saudi Arabia people speak Arab.

Preparing to Write: From Sentence to Paragraph

A paragraph is a grouping of sentences that all relate to the same topic or main idea. In this assignment, the topic is you, and the main idea is your life now.

Answer these questions in complete sentences. One example answer has been started for you.

1. What is your name? _____

2. Where are you from? _____

3. Where do you live? _____

4. What are your favorite free-time activities? *In my free time, I like to* _____

5. Where do you study? _____

6. Where are your classmates from? _____

7. How do you feel about your life now? _____

Writing a Paragraph

Now copy your answers from Preparing to Write into paragraph form. Add more information, if necessary.

→

WRITING TIP

In English, the first sentence of a paragraph usually begins five spaces to the right of the other lines. This is called **indenting.** Always **indent** your paragraphs.

Editing and Rewriting

Editing Checklist

Check the Details

1. *After you complete your paragraph, check your writing. Use this checklist.*

   ❏ Underline any country, nationality, or language words. Did you use the correct form?

   ❏ Did you indent at the beginning of the paragraph?

2. *Make your corrections. Rewrite your paragraph.*

While you are using this book, keep a notebook. Use this notebook to list and review vocabulary and grammar. You can also use it for your writing.

Vocabulary Log

What words or phrases would you like to remember from this chapter? Write five to ten items in your notebook. Be sure to include words that go together (prepositions, for example) and other forms of the words that you know. Also write a sentence using each word so that you will remember how to use your words. Here (in the notebook on the right) are a couple of examples. How can you learn the words you list? Is there anything else that you would like to add to the information in your notebook?

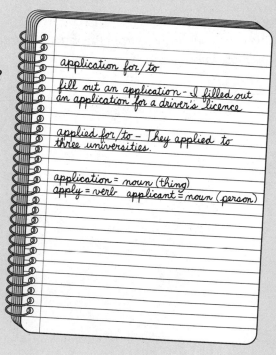

application for/to

fill out an application - I filled out an application for a driver's licence

applied for/to - They applied to three universities.

application = noun (thing)
apply = verb applicant = noun (person)

Grammar and Punctuation Review

Look over your writing from this chapter. What changes do you need to make in grammar and punctuation? Write them in your notebook. Review them before the next writing assignment.

Chapter 2

Cameos

We give information about people in many different ways. We say their names and their nationalities. We also describe the way they look. In this chapter you will read brief descriptions of people, sometimes called *cameos*, and practice using words that describe people.

Starting Point

Describing People   The following lists contain words that can describe people.

Age	Gender	Height	Physical Appearance	Hair
young	man	tall	attractive	curly
old	woman	short	funny-looking	straight
middle-aged	girl	medium-sized	average-looking	dark
	boy		unusual-looking	long
				short

1. *Work with a classmate. Match the words in the list with the people in the picture. Write the words in the boxes on the next page.*

A. Wesley Nash

_____

_____

_____

_____

C. Sonia Alvarez

_____

_____

_____

_____

B. Martha Goodkin

_____

_____

_____

_____

D. Jeff Lee

_____

_____

_____

_____

2. *Study the picture again. What jobs or activities do you think these people do? Complete the sentences with words from the list and give an explanation for your opinion.*

ANSWER KEY

homemaker   ice skater   student
musician   businessperson   teacher

a. I think Jeff Lee looks like a(n) _____ because _____

_____.

b. Wesley Nash is carrying a violin case, so I think he is a(n)

_____.

c. I think Sonia Alvarez is a(n) _____ because

_____.

d. Martha Goodkin is probably a(n) _____ because

_____.

Reading

Newspaper Clippings

The people in the picture on page 12 are famous in their community! Articles about them appeared in the local newspaper.

1. *Match these descriptions with the people in the picture on page 12.* ***Skim*** *the articles for general information. Write the names on the lines. The first one has been done for you.*

Sophia Agnew

won first prize in the Regional Figure Skating Competition... lives in Tacoma with her parents, Ed and Maria. In March,... will compete in the National Figure Skating Competition.

. . .

received a certificate for his work in the Big Brother Program. This program uses volunteers, ages 14 to 20, who spend one afternoon a week in activities with young boys. Call 555-1285 for more information.

. . .

Police in Norwood are looking for the man who robbed the City Bank on Friday. A tall, middle-aged man with a beard walked into the bank and stole $40,000 from the teller. No one was hurt in the robbery.

. . .

was honored last night for fifty years of community service... taught math and science at South Middle School. In 1965,... started the Technical Careers Program. This program matched students with people who use math and science in their jobs.

2. *Look at exercise 2 on page 13. Were you right about the jobs and activities of the people in the picture? Complete these sentences with the correct information. Use the words in the list on page 13.*

    a. Martha Goodkin is _____.

    b. Jeff Lee is _____.

    c. Sonia Alvarez is _____.

    d. Wesley Nash is _____.

3. *Go back to the newspaper descriptions given on page 14. What words helped you identify each person? Underline these words. Compare your choices with a classmate's choices. Were the words the same for both of you?*

....

In this unit you are using adjectives and nouns to describe people.

1. *Study the definitions of **noun** and **adjective**.*

Rules	Examples
A **noun** is a word that names someone or something.	Martha city time
An **adjective** is a word that gives information about a noun.	tall middle-aged funny-looking
Adjectives go before nouns or after forms of *to be*.	She is a **tall** woman. She is **young.**

Targeting

Adjectives and Nouns

2. *Read these sentences. Look at each underlined word, and decide if it is a noun or an adjective. Put a check in the correct column.*

	Noun	Adjective
a. Sophia is a <u>young</u> person.	_____	✓
b. My mother is a <u>musician</u>.	_____	_____
c. My neighbor has a <u>funny-looking</u> dog.	_____	_____
d. She is a <u>short</u> person.	_____	_____
e. We ate <u>Chinese</u> food.	_____	_____
f. Uncle Rolfe was a <u>teacher</u> for 30 years.	_____	_____
g. The <u>man</u> in the blue suit is my brother.	_____	_____
h. My roommate is from <u>Japan</u>.	_____	_____
i. She's a <u>middle-aged</u> woman.	_____	_____
j. My grandmother was a <u>homemaker</u>.	_____	_____
k. My father works in that <u>tall</u> building.	_____	_____
l. Mr. and Mrs. Po live in an <u>attractive</u> house.	_____	_____

3. *Complete this exercise using adjectives and nouns about yourself.*
   a. Describe yourself. Write three adjectives and three nouns. Two examples are done for you.

Adjectives	Nouns
kind	*a student*
_____	_____
_____	_____
_____	_____

   b. Add one false, or untrue, word to each column in part (a).
   c. Read your list to a classmate. Does he or she agree with the words in your list? Can your classmate pick out the false words?

This exercise will help you get started on the next assignment—to write about yourself!

1. *Choose paragraph (1) or (2) in the art that follows and complete the sentences. Which description would you prefer to use to describe yourself?*

1. Write a serious description of yourself.

My name is_____ .

I am a _____ from _____ .

In physical appearance, I am

_____ , _____ , and _____ .

When you first meet me, you

may be surprised to know that I

_____ .

I am studying English because

_____ . In my free time, I like

to _____ .

2. Write a funny description of yourself.

WANTED
BY
POLICE

POLICE TODAY ARE LOOKING FOR...

_____ . _____ is a

_____ (male/female) with _____ hair

and _____ eyes. Yesterday this person

_____ and _____ . (She or he) did

this because _____ . Friends say that

(she or he) _____ , but the police

_____ . If you see this person, _____

_____ .

Describe yourself. Add more information to your writing from the Preparing to Write exercise, or create your own paragraph. If you need help with adjectives and nouns, look at "Targeting: Adjectives and Nouns" in this chapter.

**Writing a Personal
Description**

Editing and Rewriting

Editing for Sentence Punctuation and Capitalization

1. *Study these rules for sentence punctuation and capitalization.*

Rules	Examples
Every sentence begins with a capital letter and ends with a period, a question mark, or an exclamation point.	**S**he is a student here. **W**here are you living**?** **I** found an apartment**!**
Names of people and places (countries, cities, streets, businesses, etc.) begin with capital letters.	We went to **L**os **A**ngeles with **F**umiko **A**rai and **M**rs. **R**odriguez.
The names of languages and nationalities, universities, schools, and colleges also begin with capital letters.	**G**abriel is studying **G**erman at **O**hio **U**niversity.

2. *Put a check (✓) in front of the three correct sentences.*

   a. _____ he is a tall man with gray hair.

   b. _____ The robber escaped from the police.

   c. _____ They are studying English for business.

   d. _____ Are they visiting london?

   e. _____ Alexander Graham Bell invented the telephone.

   f. _____ mr. lewis works at the ritz hotel.

3. *Correct the capitalization and punctuation in this paragraph. The first sentence is done for you.*

ANSWER KEY

Khalid   Al-Shafi   Kuwait.
~~khalid al shafi~~ is from ~~kuwait~~   he is studying English at boston

university   he lives in a dormitory at the university on

commonwealth avenue   his roommate's name is peter jones

peter and khalid get along very well   they have only one prob-

lem   peter likes to get up early   khalid, on the other hand,

never goes to bed before 1:00 a.m.   this is a big problem for

both students   they are thinking about changing roommates.

Editing Checklist
Check the Content

1. *Exchange your description of yourself with a classmate. After you read your classmate's description, answer the questions.*

❏ Is there enough information?
❏ Can you understand the description?

Check the Details

2. *Read your description again. If necessary, revise (change) your own writing. Try to change unclear words or sentences. Add more details, if necessary. Then continue checking your own writing. Use this checklist.*

❏ Do you begin every sentence with a capital letter and end with a period, a question mark, or an exclamation point?
❏ Are there any names of places? Do they begin with capital letters?
❏ Are the names of nationalities and countries correct? Are they capitalized?

3. *Make your corrections. Rewrite your paragraph.*

Vocabulary Log

What words or phrases would you like to remember from this chapter? Write five to ten items in your notebook. Examples are on page 10.

Grammar and Punctuation Review

Look over your writing from this chapter. What changes did you need to make in grammar and punctuation? Write them in your notebook. Review them before the next writing assignment.

Class Activity **Profiles of Classmates**

1 Write all the names of your classmates on pieces of paper. Choose a piece of paper and write a description of that person. If you need help with vocabulary, review Chapter 1 and this chapter.

2 Read your description aloud to the class, but don't say the name of the person. Ask the class to guess who the person is.

3 Make a class poster or book with the pictures and the descriptions of everyone in the class.

Chapter 3

Breaking Away

Starting Point

Sometimes people have to make difficult decisions about their living situations. This chapter deals with a problem for a student living with his family and problems with other living situations.

Living on Your Own

Different families have different expectations about how long young people continue to live at home.

Read the following situations, and check one choice for each situation. Then answer the questions in item (4). Discuss your opinions with a partner or a small group.

1. After he graduates from high school, Simon will get a job. He wants to have his own apartment, but his parents say he is too young to live alone. He will be 19 when he finishes high school.

   In my opinion, Simon should _____ stay with his parents.

   _____ live on his own.

2. Hiromi just graduated from college. She has a job and would like to move into an apartment with two friends. Her parents want her to live with them until she gets married.

   In my opinion, Hiromi should _____ stay with her parents.

   _____ live in an apartment with her friends.

3. Giao and Sam have both finished college and have good jobs. They are going to get married next year. When they get married, they plan to live with Sam's parents. Giao isn't very happy about this. She wants them to have their own home.

   In my opinion, they should _____ live with Sam's parents.

   _____ get their own place to live.

4. Are these situations typical for people you know? When do people usually move away from home? Do married couples usually live on their own or with one person's parents?

Reading

A Place to Call Your Own

This reading concerns a student's decision about living on his own—without the help of his family.

1. *Read the following selection.*

A Place to Call Your Own

[1] Van Ly lives with his family in a three-bedroom apartment. There are five children, so Van has to share a room with two younger brothers. When Van was younger, he didn't mind sharing his bedroom, but now he goes to Highline Community College, and he really wants his own room. It is very difficult for him because he doesn't have a quiet place to study.

[2] Van works at a restaurant and makes about $300 a week. He eats breakfast at home and takes food with him for lunch. He eats dinner at the restaurant for free. His expenses are bus fare, clothing, tuition, textbooks, and occasional activities with his friends. Van is trying to decide if he can afford to move out of his parents' apartment.

[3] Here are some advertisements for apartments near Highline Community College.

1 MONTH FREE! CLEAN AND CONVENIENT! Next to H.C.C. 1 bdrm in Midway/ Des Moines area. $370-$390 mo. 555-9773	AD #351. $99 Move-In Special! DesMoines area, 2 bdrm, fireplace, washer/dryer hookups. $495. Zara/Smith & Associates. 941-5555	**Highline Court** The perfect place to live. 1 bdrm currently available. $425 mo. Call today. 870-5555

2. *Answer these questions.*

    a. What do you think these words from the advertisements mean?

       H.C.C. *Highline Community College*

       $425 mo _____

       bdrm _____

b. Why do you think Van wants his own room? What is the basic problem?

_____

_____

c. Can Van afford to move into an apartment?

_____

d. Does he have any other possibilities?

_____

e. What do you think is best for Van? _____ _I think he should_ _____

_____

3. *Now analyze what two experts say about this situation. Decide if you agree or disagree with each of them. Write your opinion on the next page.*

ANSWER KEY

EXPERT 1 *(A Financial Planner)*

Ly Van should try to work with what he has. He cannot afford to live on his own. Besides rent, he would need to pay for breakfast and lunch, gas, water, and electricity. He would also need to buy furniture.

Why can't Van find a quiet space in his apartment? His family should help him with this.

Van needs to make some changes, but he should try to save his money, not spend it. ◄

. . . . .

EXPERT 2 *(A Psychologist)*

Is there another reason that Ly Van wants to have his own space? If he works in the evening at a restaurant and takes classes in the daytime, he probably isn't at home very much. Why can't he study at the college library before he goes to work in the evening? Then he would just go home to sleep at the same time as everyone else in the family.

Perhaps Van wants to be more independent or to have more privacy. He should try to work this out with his family first before he moves out on his own. ◄

a. What is Expert 1's basic advice about money? Underline it in the reading. Do you agree or disagree?

_____

b. What does Expert 2 think the basic problem is? Underline it in the reading. Do you agree that this may be the problem?

_____

Targeting

Collocations

When you learn new words, it often helps to study what words go together—**collocations.**

1. *Study these expressions.*

Expressions	*Examples*
make [a certain amount of money]	He **makes $300** a week.
spend [a certain amount of money] **on/for** [something]	They **spend $600 on/for rent** each month.
[something] **costs** [a certain amount of money]	**Lunch** usually **costs about $5** at the cafeteria.
[something] **costs** [someone] [a certain amount of money]	**Rent costs me $400** a month.
It costs [a certain amount of money] **for** [something]	**It costs $400 for rent.**
It costs [a certain amount of money] **to** [do something]	**It costs $2.50 to take the bus** each day.
afford [something]	She can't **afford a new car.**
afford to [verb]	I can't **afford to buy** any new clothes right now.
share [something]	The three boys **share a bedroom.**
share [something] **with** [someone]	I **share my apartment with two other people.**

2. *Complete the sentences with words from the chart above. You may need more than one word in each blank.*

(ANSWER KEY)

    a. How much does it _____ rent an apartment?

    b. I'm saving my money to buy textbooks in August, so I can't

        _____ buy any new clothes now.

    c. In my part-time job, I _____ about $60 a week.

    d. Fairly good used cars probably _____ about $4,000.

    e. I usually _____ about $4 _____ lunch.

    f. When I can _____ it, I would like to have my own

        apartment.

    g. It _____ $50 a month _____ a bus pass.

    h. Our apartments are very similar, but I spend more money

        _____ rent than my brother does.

3. *Write some sentences about your expenses. Use words from exercises 1 and 2.*

_____

_____

_____

_____

_____

Writing

Preparing to Write 1: Quickwriting

Sometimes it is difficult to decide what to write. **Quickwriting** is a way to help you get ideas about a topic.

1. *Think about these questions:*

   a. When do people you know usually move away from home?
   b. Do married couples usually live on their own or with one person's parents?
   c. What kinds of problems do people have when they want to change their living situations?

2. *In your notebook, write for five to ten minutes about "breaking away" or changing your living situation. Use some ideas from your discussion in exercise 1 to help get you started.*

Preparing to Write 2: Introductory Sentences

The first sentence of a paragraph often introduces your topic and helps the reader understand your main point.

1. *The four paragraphs below are missing their first sentences. Find a sentence from the list below. Use each sentence once. Write it at the beginning of the appropriate paragraph.* Note: *These are incomplete paragraphs.*

   • Married couples usually want to live on their own.
   • It is important for young people to experience living on their own.
   • Sometimes young people and parents have different ideas about when the young people will move away from home.
   • It costs a lot to live on your own.

   a. _____.

      This is a difficult situation. Often, the parents are hurt when their children want to leave home, and it is difficult for young people to explain why they want to leave. My sister was the first to leave our family. There was a big fight about it, and my mother was sad for months. She still worries about her. . . .

b. _____.

However, in my family, the first son and his wife always live with his parents. My father was the first son. He didn't mind living with his parents, but my mother didn't like it at all. . . .

c. _____.

A lot of people live with their parents because it is less expensive. However, there are some ways to save money. For example, it doesn't cost as much if you share an apartment. . . .

d. _____.

Living on their own gives young people an opportunity to make decisions and manage their money. They miss their families and they make mistakes, but these things are part of becoming an adult. I am living away from my family now, and I am learning a lot about. . . .

2. *The writers of the paragraphs in exercise 1 use examples to **support** their ideas. Look at the incomplete paragraphs in exercise 1 again. Underline the main ideas, and then put a checkmark (✓) by the examples.*

3. *Go back to your quickwrite (see page 26). Can you find a sentence that would be a good introductory sentence for a paragraph? Write it here, or write a new one here.*

_____

_____

Write a paragraph about breaking away or changing your living situation. Begin with your introductory sentence from the quickwrite exercise. Continue your paragraph with your ideas and examples.

Writing a Paragraph with an Introductory Sentence

Editing and Rewriting

Editing Checklist

Check the Content

1. *Exchange your paragraph with a classmate's paragraph. After you read your classmate's paragraph, answer the questions in the checklist.*

   ❏ Is there an introductory sentence to introduce the ideas?
   ❏ Is there enough information? Can you understand the ideas? Are the examples clear?

Check the Details

2. *Read your own writing again. If necessary, revise your writing. Give more information, or rewrite your introductory sentence. Then continue checking your own writing. Use the questions in the checklist.*

   ❏ Did you use any of the collocations on page 24. Check any words you used with *spend, make, cost, afford,* and *share.*
   ❏ Does every sentence begin with a capital letter and end with a period, a question mark, or an exclamation point?

3. *Make your corrections. Rewrite your paragraph.*

Vocabulary Log

What words or phrases would you like to remember from this chapter? Write five to ten items in your notebook. Examples are on page 10.

Grammar and Punctuation Review

Look over your writing from this chapter. What changes did you need to make in grammar and punctuation? Write them in your notebook. Review them before the next writing assignment.

2 Where in the World?

Even if you don't travel a lot, it's fun to think about traveling! Where would you like to go? How would you like to travel? The world is full of exciting places to explore. The topics in this section will get you thinking about some real and imaginary opportunities.

These are some of the activities you will do in this unit:

- Read about adventure travel
- Write descriptions of places
- Read charts about places to stay
- Write a fax to request information
- Write a travel brochure
- Write a postcard

Chapter 4

Adventure Travel

What kind of travel are you familiar with? A visit to a new city? A bus trip? A trip to someplace far away? In this chapter you will read about different types of travel and practice a lot of new vocabulary in your writing.

Starting Point

Vacation Variety

The travel descriptions below tell you about places to go for a vacation.

1. ***Skim*** *the descriptions on the next page, and match them with the photos below.*

City

Beach

Mountain Climbing

Park

River Rafting

Bus Tour

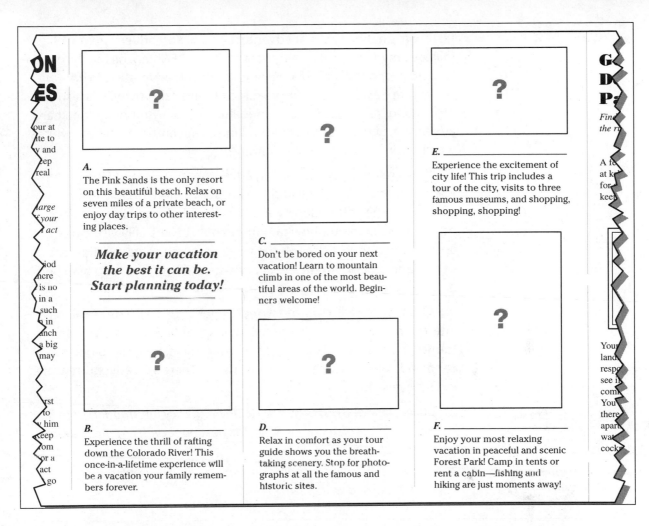

our at
te to
y and
eep
real

arge
your
act

iod
here
is no
in a
such
in
nch
a big
may

rst
to
him
eep
om
or a
act
go

A. _____

The Pink Sands is the only resort on this beautiful beach. Relax on seven miles of a private beach, or enjoy day trips to other interesting places.

Make your vacation the best it can be. Start planning today!

B. _____

Experience the thrill of rafting down the Colorado River! This once-in-a-lifetime experience will be a vacation your family remembers forever.

C. _____

Don't be bored on your next vacation! Learn to mountain climb in one of the most beautiful areas of the world. Beginners welcome!

D. _____

Relax in comfort as your tour guide shows you the breathtaking scenery. Stop for photographs at all the famous and historic sites.

E. _____

Experience the excitement of city life! This trip includes a tour of the city, visits to three famous museums, and shopping, shopping, shopping!

F. _____

Enjoy your most relaxing vacation in peaceful and scenic Forest Park! Camp in tents or rent a cabin—fishing and hiking are just moments away!

G
D
Pa

Fin
the ru

A f
at k
for
keep

Your
land
resp
see i
com
You
there
apart
wa
cock

2. *In each description in exercise 1, underline the key words that tell you what photo it matches. Compare your words with a classmate's key words. Are they the same?*

....

Reading

This selection describes a certain kind of travel.

Adventure Travel

1. *Read the description and pay attention to the key information.*

Adventure Travel

[1] Adventure travel is very popular today with people of all ages. In adventure travel, people do outdoor activities in faraway places.

[2] There are two types of adventure travel. **Soft** adventure travel includes mild physical activity. It is fairly safe. Fishing, hiking, bird watching, and trail riding are examples of soft adventure. **Hard** adventure travel includes more difficult physical activity. It is also more dangerous. You need to prepare and train your body for a hard adventure. Some examples of this kind of adventure travel are white-water rafting and mountain climbing.

[3] Why are people interested in adventure travel now? One reason is a new interest in nature and the outdoors. More people live in cities now. They often don't want to spend their vacations visiting other cities, no matter how famous. People can usually visit cities and common tourist sites on their own. Adventure travel offers the opportunity for exciting, new experiences, all with the help of experienced guides.

[4] Communities all over the world are taking advantage of the new interest in adventure travel. Small towns that had nothing to offer tourists before are now promoting hiking tours, rock climbing, and canoe rides down alligator-infested rivers. There's an adventure waiting for everyone . . . somewhere.

2. *When you **take notes**, you write down the key information from a reading. Complete the chart on the next page with key information from "Adventure Travel."*

3. *Look at the vacation photos on page 30. Find examples of adventure travel and write them below.*

Adventure Travel- _Outdoor_ activities in _____ places	
_____ adventure travel • fishing • _____ • _____ • _____ • _____	_____ adventure travel • white-water rafting • _____
Reasons for adventure travel's popularity: • a new interest in _____ by people who live in _____ • the opportunity for _____ with the help of _____	
Many _____ taking advantage of adventure travel's popularity.	

4. *Imagine that you have ten days for a vacation and enough money for a trip. Where would you like to go? Write 1, 2, and 3 below to show your top three choices.*

_____ hiking or skiing in the mountains

_____ to a big city

_____ to a beautiful, quiet beach

_____ to as many places as possible in another country

_____ nowhere

_____

(other—your choice)

5. *Is your classmate interested in adventure travel? Discuss your choices in exercise 4 with a classmate. Use these sentences to help you.*

I would like to go . . .   *or*   . . . How about you?

Think about the first choice you made in exercise 4. Why is this travel option interesting to you? Is it a dream or a real possibility? Explain why. Write for five or ten minutes in your notebook.

Quickwriting: Travel Choices

WRITING TIP

When you **quickwrite**, do not use a dictionary. If you don't know the word in English, write it in your own language.

Targeting

Adjectives to Describe Places

An **adjective** is a word that gives information about a noun. You identified adjectives in Chapter 2, page 16. We use adjectives to describe places. This section gives you choices of adjectives to help you write a description of a place.

1. *Match the adjectives in the left column with their opposites.*

   a. beautiful   _b_ boring

   b. exciting   ___ dangerous

   c. hard   ___ indoor

   d. outdoor   ___ nearby

   e. quiet   ___ soft

   f. remote   ___ ugly

   g. safe   ___ busy and noisy

2. *Make complete sentences to describe a place. Circle one choice in each column. Think about the meaning of the words you choose. Not every combination will make sense!*

Enjoy Experience the Relax at the	beautiful breathtaking outdoor peaceful physical exciting	activities peacefulness resort scenery thrill excitement	at _____! *(name of place)*	
This	adventure beautiful breathtaking outdoor peaceful physical exciting	resort tour experience beach	has includes	fishing rafting skiing _____ _____ _____ *(your ideas)*	and _____ _____ *(your ideas)*

3. *Write your sentences from exercise 2 on the lines below.*

_____

_____

_____

_____

_____

_____

_____

_____

Vocabulary Log

What words or phrases would you like to remember from this chapter? Write five to ten items in your notebook. Examples are on page 10.

Chapter 5

Decisions, Decisions

Travelers have to make a lot of choices. This chapter gives you practice reading information about places to stay and ways to travel. You will also write a fax about places to stay.

Starting Point

Places to Stay

When you travel, you need to make decisions about a place to stay.

1. *Read the information about these places to stay.*

Vancouver Youth Hostel

Single rooms	$45
Dormitory	$20

All guests have to clean up after themselves. The hostel has a kitchen.

Rose's Bed and Breakfast

Single	$ 75
Double	$ 90
Cottage	$115

All rooms have shared baths. Includes breakfast.

Bayview Hotel

	Standard	Deluxe (with view)
Single	$ 90	$120
Double	$100	$130

There is a restaurant in the hotel.

Canadian Home Stay

Placement	$150
Daily	$ 20

Includes breakfast and dinner.

2. *Look again at the ads for each place to stay. Now, give your opinion in each of these situations.*

	Place	**Cost**

a. Carlos Garcia is traveling by bicycle around Canada. He is trying not to spend very much money. Which place is best for him? What is the cost for one night?   _____ _____

b. Henri and Michelle are planning their honeymoon. Which place is best for them? What is the cost for five nights?   _____ _____

c. Your parents are coming to visit for one week. Which place is best for them? What is the cost?   _____ _____

d. You are going to stay in Vancouver for three months to study English. Which place is possible for you? What is the cost?   _____ _____

3. *Complete these sentences. Find words in exercise 1 or 2 with the meaning of the words in parentheses.*

ANSWER KEY

a. They do not have separate rooms for each visitor, just a

   ____*dormitory*____ for men and another one for women.
   (large place for a number of people to sleep)

b. The _____ rate is $20.   (everyday)

c. I am traveling by myself. I need a _____ room.   (for one person)

d. The cost _____ two meals a day.   (has as part of it)

e. In each hallway there was a _____ bathroom. (used by more than one person)

f. A _____ bed is big enough for two people.   (for two)

g. What is the _____ for two nights?   (price)

h. I have some money to _____ on small gifts to take home to my family and friends.   (pay out)

i. I am _____ to stay for three nights.   (thinking about for the future)

Vacation Information Chart

When you plan a trip, you often see charts like the one below. This chart gives information about the costs of different kinds of vacations.

Read the chart and answer the questions.

Rate per Person/ Double Occupancy	Season	Holidays without Airfare		8 days/7 nights Holidays with Airfare Included
Room Type		**2 Nights**	**Extra Night**	
Garden view	Reg	$134	$49	$630
	Peak	$144	$58	$669
Ocean view	Reg	$158	$64	$765
	Peak	$175	$70	$800

Regular Season: January 1 through January 19, April through December 18
Peak Season: January 20 through March 31, December 19 through December 31

READING TIP

Look first at the **headings** on the top line(s) of the chart. They tell what the chart is going to show.

1. Are these rates for the room or for each person? _____

2. What is the cost of the least expensive trip with airfare included? _____

3. What is *Reg* short for? _____

4. Is December 25 during the regular or peak season? _____

5. How much does a garden view room cost for two nights during the regular season? _____

6. How much does the same room cost for two nights in February? _____

7. How much does an ocean view room cost, with airfare, for an eight-day vacation in March? _____

8. Nick and Connie are planning their honeymoon for June 11 through June 18. They have $2,500 to spend. They will need about $50 a day for food. Can they stay in an ocean view room?

_____

Travel on a Budget

Many tourists are interested in spending as little money as possible when they travel. Are you like that? Here is some information about ways to travel cheaply.

1. *Read the following selection.*

Travel on a Budget

[1] If you don't have a big budget, what are some cheap ways to travel? In the 1960s, a lot of people hitchhiked in the United States. They stood at the side of the road, stuck out their thumbs, and hoped for a ride going their way. Nowadays, however, very few people want to take a chance and ride with strangers.

[2] However, there are still a few "almost free" ways to travel. One is to drive a car for a car transportation company. When people move from one part of the country to another, they often need to move their cars, but they don't want to drive them themselves. They pay a transportation company to do this for them. Some transportation companies put cars on trailers to move them. Other companies hire people to drive them. The drivers usually have to make a deposit and pay for gas, but this is a great way to travel if you can find a car going your way. A bigger problem is how to get back home!

[3] How about a free plane ride? If you can fly with almost no advance notice, you can be a courier for a mailing and package delivery company. A courier delivers something in a hurry. The company may buy you a round-trip plane ticket if you deliver a package for them. There are even companies that need to make large mailings internationally. Because it's so expensive to send international mail, these companies pay for someone to fly overseas with boxes of letters for their offices or customers in other countries. A free international trip—now there's a great deal!

[4] If these possibilities don't work for you, remember that you can save money if you plan your trip far in advance. There are three ways to get the cheapest airfares ("discount" fares): (1) buy your ticket two or three weeks in advance; (2) travel in the middle of the week; and (3) buy a round-trip ticket. Bus tickets, train tickets, and rental cars are also cheaper when you can make your reservations far ahead of your trip.

2. *Complete the sentences with one of these words from the reading. You will need to use one word more than once.*

advance	discount	stranger(s)
deliver	reservations	trailer
deposit	round-trip	transportation
		way(s)

a. Which _____*way*_____ are you going? Can I get a ride with you?

b. There are three _____ to solve this problem.

c. People you don't know are _____.

d. Airplanes, cars, buses, trucks, and trains are all types of

_____.

e. A car or truck sometimes pulls a _____ to carry something.

f. If you want to reserve a hotel room and you arrive after

6:00 p.m., you have to have a credit card or make a _____ for the cost of a one-night stay.

g. Some people like planning trips many months in _____.

h. I don't want a _____ ticket. I am only going one way.

i. An overnight mailing company promises to _____ a package by the next day.

j. The regular price was $100, but with the 10 percent

_____, I paid only $90.

k. I made _____ two weeks ago, but they haven't sent me my tickets yet.

3. *Inexpensive ways to travel are often far from perfect. Analyze the reading. Identify the problems with each of these options.*

Hitchhiking   _____

_____

_____

Driving for a car transportation company   _____

_____

_____

Traveling as a courier   _____

_____

_____

Traveling with discount fares   _____

_____

_____

4. *Can you think of any other travel problems* not *in the reading? Add them to exercise 3.*

5. *Would any of these budget travel options work for you? Why or why not? Discuss your ideas with a partner or a small group.*

Targeting

Nouns and Verbs

Nouns and verbs are the basis of English sentences.

1. *Study these facts about nouns and verbs.*

Rules	Examples
A **noun** is a word that names someone or something.	student hotel Vancouver
A **verb** is a word that expresses action, perception, or relationship.	go feel be
Verbs change tense (form) to show when things happen.	I **am studying** English now I **will study** French next year.
Be careful with the article *a* before a singular count noun. Remember that *a* changes to *an* before a vowel sound.	**a** box **an** adventure **a** place **an** ugly place
The *u* in some words is pronounced "you" instead of "uh." This is not a vowel sound.	**an u**nhappy person (uh) **a u**nited group of people (you)

2. *Some words can be both a noun and a verb. Are the words in **boldface** nouns or verbs? Put a check in the correct column.*

		Noun	Verb
a.	Hotels in the center of the city **cost** more.	____	✓
b.	What is the **cost** for one night?	____	____
c.	Adventure **travel** is becoming very popular.	____	____
d.	I like to **travel.**	____	____
e.	Canadian Home **Stay** is the name of an organization.	____	____
f.	We will **stay** two nights in Toronto.	____	____

	Noun	**Verb**

g. I would like to **experience** the thrill of parachuting, but I know I will never do it. I'm afraid of heights. ____ ____

h. We had a terrible **experience** on our trip. ____ ____

i. The tour buses always **stop** in front of our house because President Kennedy was born in the house next door. ____ ____

j. They have planned a short **stop** in Calgary, Alberta. ____ ____

k. My parents arranged their **visit** to take place during the Mardi Gras celebrations. ____ ____

l. The class arranged to **visit** a museum. ____ ____

m. Adventure trips **offer** exciting, new travel possibilities. ____ ____

n. The tour guide's **offer** to help carry my suitcase was nice. ____ ____

3. *Write* **a** *or* **an** *if necessary before the nouns in these sentences. Write* X *if you don't need an article.*

ANSWER KEY

a. I need to get _____ entry visa to travel there.

b. Please send me _____ brochure about your hotel.

c. We had _____ exciting trip.

d. We saw _____ many beautiful places.

e. I live in _____ apartment here.

f. Is there _____ indoor swimming pool at your hotel?

g. I am _____ university student.

h. I went on _____ trip to Washington, D.C.

i. I would like to make _____ reservation.

j. There is _____ entry fee at the park.

k. Then _____ terrible thing happened.

l. We saw _____ animals alongside the road in the park.

Writing

....

Preparing to Write: Writing Requests

To make reservations for your trip, you will need to request information.

Complete the requests for information. Use one of these expressions for each request.

I'd like to . . .	Please send/tell me . . .
How/What/Where . . .	Do/Does . . .

1. __I'd like to__ receive more information about things to do in your area.

2. _____ a brochure with more information.

3. _____ visit your area in March.

4. _____ is the weather like in March?

5. _____ more about your hotel.

6. _____ much would a week's stay in a double room cost?

7. _____ is the closest airport?

8. _____ make a reservation for a single room for two nights.

9. _____ you have cooking facilities in the rooms?

Writing a Fax to Request Information

These travel ads give you choices for a vacation.

1. *Read the following ads. Choose one of these places to visit.*

HAWAII

Visit a special place in Hawaii...

GRAND WAILEA RESORT
Hotel and Spa

3850 Wailea Alanui Drive, Wailea, Maui HI 96753

Tel: 808-875-1234   Fax: 808-874-5143

BALI
Intercontinental Resort
on Jimbaran Beach

Jalan Uluwatu No. 45,
Jimbaran 80361, Bali
Indonesia

e-mail: dpsha@interconti.com
TEL: (62 361) 701 888   FAX: (62 361) 701 777

Abigail's
HOTEL
906 McClure Street, Victoria, B.C.

TEL: 250-388-5363
FAX: 250-388-7787

e-mail:
inkeeper@abigailshotel.com

2. *Work with a partner. Complete this fax about the vacation place you chose. What information will you need?*

WRITING TIP

People often use **block style** for formal writing. Instead of indenting at the beginning of a paragraph, they put two spaces between paragraphs.

—FAX—

DATE: _____

TO: _____

FAX NUMBER: _____

FROM: _____

MESSAGE

I am interested in getting more information about _____
_____ . Please _____
me _____ . I will be traveling _____ ,
so I need to know the rates for _____ .
Do you require a deposit?

I am interested in visiting from _____
to _____ . _____
_____
(add another question or statement)
I will be arriving by _____ . Please send me
(kind of transportation)
_____ about how to get to your location from
_____ .

My address is: _____
_____
_____

My telephone number is: _____

Thank you.

45

Editing and Rewriting

Editing Checklist

Check the Content

1. *Exchange your fax with a classmate's. After you read your classmate's fax, answer this question.*

   ❏ Is the information clear and complete?

Check the Details

2. *Read your fax again. If necessary, revise what you wrote. Change or add information, as necessary. Then continue checking your own writing. Use this question.*

   ❏ Did you write your family name last?

3. *Make your corrections and rewrite your fax on a separate piece of paper. If you want, send it off!*

Vocabulary Log

What words or phrases would you like to remember from this chapter? Write five to ten items in your notebook. Examples are on page 10.

Grammar and Punctuation Review

Look over your writing from this chapter. What changes did you need to make in grammar and punctuation? Write them in your notebook. Review them before the next writing assignment.

People use a lot of interesting vocabulary to talk or write about their trips. In this chapter you will read postcards and write one yourself.

Wish You Were Here

Starting Point

....

Many people send postcards to friends and family from their vacation places.

Postcards

1. *Read these postcards.*

2. *What do you know about Geri's trip from her postcard? Write the letter of the correct answer in each sentence.*

(ANSWER KEY)

a. Geri __b__ traveling alone.
   a. is   **b.** is not

b. Geri likes the scenery in _____.
   a. Kansas   **b.** Colorado

c. The bus ride was _____.
   a. boring   **b.** incredible

d. In both places, the people were _____.
   a. interesting   **b.** nice

e. Geri _____ the dormitory.
   a. likes   **b.** doesn't like

f. Geri's last name is probably _____.
   a. Taylor   **b.** Turner

Reading

Space Travel

What's left for the adventurous tourist to do? How about a trip to outer space?

1. *Read this selection.*

Space Travel

[1] Will you ever get a postcard from space? Some people hope so! They have formed a group called the X-Prize Foundation. The group's leader, Peter Diamandis, is trying to get companies to develop space tours. He hopes to put together a $10 million prize—the X-Prize—for the first flights that take tourists at least sixty miles into space.

[2] The company that develops the first tourist flights will face a lot of challenges. One of the first challenges for tourism in space is the spacecraft. It has to be affordable and reusable. It also has to be safe. Then, once in space, finding a good tourist destination is also a challenge. It takes *light years* for objects in space to travel from place to place, but most tourists have only a week or two. A trip to the moon would take only three days, but what an uncomfortable three days those would be! So far, no one has developed a first-class section in a spacecraft.

[3] Would tourists really want to go to the moon? The moon has no atmosphere, so it doesn't have any sound or blue sky. A night on the moon is two weeks long and has an average temperature of minus 240 degrees Fahrenheit (–240°F). The average daytime temperature on the moon is hot enough to boil water on Earth. Unfortunately, there is no water on the moon.

[4] With so many problems, there may not be too many people interested at first. However, with so few unexplored places on Earth, space offers a unique opportunity to experience something different and exciting. Right now, the only space trips are for research. But who knows what the future will bring?

2. *Find words in the reading with the same meaning and write them on the lines.*

ANSWER KEY

a. director   _leader_

b. plan, build, start   _____

c. award   _____

d. movement through the air or the atmosphere   _____

e. difficult tasks with problems to solve   _____

f. vehicle for travel in space   _____

g. inexpensive, easy to pay for   _____

h. able to be used again   _____

i. not dangerous   _____

j. place someone is going to   _____

k. a measure of time in space   _____

l. very high quality   _____

m. the gases that surround Earth   _____

n. different from all others, one of a kind   _____

3. *Answer these questions about the reading.*

ANSWER KEY

a. Is there travel to space now? _____

b. What are three adjectives that tell what a spacecraft for

tourism needs to be? _____

Which of the words is most important for a tourist who is

thinking about traveling to the moon? _____

c. To win the X-Prize, does a company have to send tourists all

the way to the moon? _____

d. Can people breathe air on the moon? _____

e. Would tourists want to go to the moon? Why or why not?

_____

Reflect on Reading

In exercise 3, some of the information was clear and easy to find in the reading. To find other, more difficult information, you had to **analyze** the reading, or study it closely. This is a very important reading skill.

Circle the answers to the questions below.

What questions were easy?

a   b (part 1)   b (part 2)   c   d   e

For which questions did you already know the answer from your own knowledge?

a   b (part 1)   b (part 2)   c   d   e

For which questions did you have to analyze the reading?

a   b (part 1)   b (part 2)   c   d   e

4.   *Would you want to go into space? To the moon? Why or why not? Discuss this with a partner or a small group.*

Targeting

. . . .

Adjectives to Describe an Experience

Writers use adjectives to tell about their travel experiences. Some adjectives show if the experience is positive and fun or negative and unpleasant. Other adjectives are neutral—not positive or negative.

1.   *Go back to the postcards on page 47. Circle the adjectives.*

2. Look at each adjective in the left column. Decide if it is positive, negative, or neutral. (Note: Some may be both positive or negative.)
Write the adjective in the correct column(s).

The View

	Positive	Negative	Neutral
beautiful	*beautiful*	_____	_____
incredible	_____	_____	_____
interesting	_____	_____	_____
nice	_____	_____	_____
typical	_____	_____	_____
uninteresting	_____	_____	_____

The Experience of Traveling

boring	_____	_____	_____
challenging	_____	_____	_____
cold	_____	_____	_____
depressing	_____	_____	_____
exciting	_____	_____	_____
uncomfortable	_____	_____	_____
hot	_____	_____	_____
relaxing	_____	_____	_____
tiring	_____	_____	_____
wonderful	_____	_____	_____

3. Complete these sentences with adjectives from the list in exercise 2.

a. This mountain climbing trip is very *challenging* .

b. A trip to the desert would be _____ .

c. I stayed at home on my last vacation. It was _____ .

d. The scenery in the mountains is _____ .

e. The beach was _____ , but when we went into

the city, there were a lot of very poor people. It was very

_____ .

f. The airplane trip was _____ because it was windy
and bumpy.

g. It was an eighteen-hour trip, and the scenery was not very

spectacular. It was _____ .

4. *Work with a partner. Student A, look at the vocabulary in exercise 2
on page 51. Read any five words to your partner. Do not look at this
page. Student B, fill in the five words in the description below. Does
it make any sense?*

   Come to _____ Beach Harbor Resort! Enjoy

_____ sunsets and _____ nights in a

_____ hotel by the _____ beach.

   *Student B, look at the vocabulary in exercise 2 on page 51. Read any
five words to your partner. Do not look at this page. Student A, fill in
the five words in the description below. Does it make any sense?*

   We're having a _____ time. The hotel is _____

and _____ . Tomorrow, we are going on a _____

trip to a _____ historical site. Wish you were here!

5. *Work with a partner. Fill in adjectives for this postcard from space.*

   We're having a _____ time. When we took off

into space, I was _____ . This spacecraft is

_____ , the view is _____ . Wish you
   (but / and)
were here!

Writing

Always write addresses in the format accepted by the post office. Addresses in the United States follow the format below.

Preparing to Write: Address Format

1. *Study these forms of addresses.*

Forms of addresses in the United States:
- The names of people, streets, and places are capitalized.
- The titles **Mr., Mrs.,** or **Ms.** are usually not required.
- If you use a job title, it follows the name:

Jean Taylor   *or*   Jean Taylor, Director

Director   English Language Program

English Language Program

Example:

Mr./Mrs./Ms. First Name Last Name   Mr. and Mrs. Michael Rivkin

Street Address   294 Kent Street, #4

City, State Zip Code   San Francisco, CA 94104

> **WRITING TIP**
>
> Each country has a different style for writing addresses. Try to copy addresses exactly as you see them in brochures on on letterhead paper or envelopes.

2. *Correct the mistakes in these addresses.*

a. M̶s̶. Ann Smith (M)
145 Chance Lane
Philadelphia, PA 19101

b. Mrs. Jones, Tom
Decatur street
Federal Way, WA 98023

c. Mr. and Mrs. Arturo Lopez
13300 Noel Rd.
dallas, texas 75240

d. President Peter Schmidt
Republic Lending company
20 Washington Ave. south
Minneapolis, MN 55401

e. Dr. Allen Shellinger
west broadway 110
New York, NY 10017

f. lois laney
40 Larchmont St.
Chicago, IL 60675

g. Goodman, Jane
Technology Square
Westlake, OH 44145

h. Alex and Nancy Price
700 Anderson hill Rd.
St. Louis, Missouri 63102

i. mrs Francine Billings
107 Selden St.
San Diego, CA
92117

j. G. De Angelis
Spring Street Menlo Park
CA 96025

ANSWER KEY

6. *Write these names and addresses on the envelopes.*

a. Mark lives on 25th Avenue. His house number is 9500. His last name is Hammond. The zip code for Columbus is 43202. Columbus is in Ohio.

b. Rita Hernandez is the director of marketing at the Crane Company in Miami. The company is on NW 107th Ave. at number 4200. The zip code in this area of Florida is 33172.

You are on vacation and you want to write a postcard to someone.

Complete this postcard. Address it to someone in the United States or Canada. If you don't know anyone else to address it to, send it to the authors of this book: Anita Sökmen and Daphne Mackey, (ESL Authors), Houghton Mifflin Company, College Division, 222 Berkeley St., Boston, MA 02116. Use some of the adjectives from this unit in your description. Use separate paper if you need more space.

Greetings from the World Traveler

TO:

_____

_____

_____

_____

"*Greetings from The World Traveler*". Copyright © 1998 Designs, Inc., Chicago, IL.

Editing and Rewriting

You will use the present and present progressive tenses frequently in your writing.

1. *Review the rules on the following page for using the simple present and present progressive tenses.*

Editing for Simple Present and Present Progressive

Rules	Examples
Use the **simple present tense** to show habits, general truths, or facts.	The mountains **are** beautiful. International students **live** in a special dormitory.
Use the **present progressive** tense to show something happening now or something temporary.	We **are looking** for an apartment. I'**m staying** with friends right now.

> For more information about **spelling rules for adding endings,** see page 198 in Reference.

2. *Put a check (✓) in front of the correct sentences.*

a. _____ What are you doing right now?

b. _____ The train almost always is leaving on time.

c. _____ I'm looking for a place to stay.

d. _____ The bus tour of the mountain usually is taking four hours.

e. _____ A double room at the Ambassador Hotel costs $80.

f. _____ We stay with friends for now.

g. _____ The travel guide is usually saying "Don't worry!" just before we have a big problem.

3. *Correct the mistakes in the incorrect sentences in exercise 2. Write the revised sentences here.*

_____

_____

_____

_____

_____

Editing Checklist

Check the Content

1. *Exchange your postcard with a classmate. After you read your classmate's postcard, answer these questions.*

    ❏ Is the message clear?
    ❏ Are there enough adjectives to describe the place?

Check the Details

2. *Read your own postcard again. Keep in mind the questions in exercise 1. If necessary, revise what you wrote. Add more information or change some vocabulary. Then continue checking your own writing. Ask these questions.*

    ❏ Did you use the present tense for general truths, facts, and habits?
    ❏ Did you use the present progressive tense for temporary or continuous activities?
    ❏ Does every sentence begin with a capital letter and end with a period, a question mark, or an exclamation point?
    ❏ Look at the address. Is it in the correct form?

3. *Make your corrections. Rewrite your postcard on a separate piece of paper.*

Vocabulary Log

What words or phrases would you like to remember from this chapter? Write five to ten items in your notebook. Examples are on page 10.

Grammar and Punctuation Review

Look over your writing from this chapter. What changes did you need to make in grammar and punctuation? Write them in your notebook. Review them before the next writing assignment.

Chapter 7

Travel Highlights

In this chapter you will read about a travel experience and write a travel brochure. Writing the brochure will give you an opportunity to use the travel vocabulary in this unit.

Starting Point

Appealing Places

Travel agents display many travel brochures in their offices. These brochures tell you the most exciting things about places.

1. *Look at the example brochure below. Discuss these questions about it with a classmate.*

   a. Is this an interesting brochure?
   b. What do you notice most about it?
   c. Do you want to visit this place?

TRAVEL THE WORLD
City Tours International, Inc.

VISIT SCENIC BOSTON!

'Relax in one of the most beautiful cities in America!

'Stroll the park's winding walks among flower beds and fountains.'

'See famous Farmer's Market in the heart of the city with it's tantalizing selection of food from around the world.'

'You won't want to miss the bus tour of the famous Historic District.'

2. *Look at the headings above each photograph and description in the brochure. List the verbs, adjectives, and nouns in the headings.*

READING TIP

Headings are usually separated from the rest of the information. They are often in bigger type or *italics* or **boldface**. Look at the headings first. They help you understand what is in a reading.

Verbs	Adjectives	Nouns
_____	_____	_____
_____	_____	_____
_____	_____	_____

Writing

Preparing to Write: Organizing Information

Imagine you work for a company that publishes travel brochures. Your job is to write a travel brochure about a vacation place. It can be a city, a country, a lake, or a park—choose any place you want.

1. *Answer these questions to help plan your brochure.*

The name of the place or area is _____.

a. What are the most interesting *places* to visit in this area?

_____   _____   _____

_____   _____   _____

b. What are some fun *activities* to do in this place?

_____   _____   _____

_____   _____   _____

c. What *pictures* will you need for your brochure?

_____   _____   _____

2. *Write some possibilities for **titles** for the front of the brochure. Some titles are started for you.*

BEAUTIFUL _____

VISIT _____

A WORLD/CITY/AREA OF _____

_____

(another idea)

3. Write some possible **headings** for different sections of the brochure.

_____

_____

_____

Writing a Travel Brochure

You need a description for each place and activity in your brochure. If you need help as you write your descriptions, look again at the brochure on page 58.

1. What things will your brochure feature? Choose two or three places or activities to include. Write a description (about three sentences) of each place or activity. Use some of the adjectives, verbs, and nouns in this unit. Continue on a separate piece of paper if you need more space.

WRITING TIP

Try to use active verbs, such as _visit, enjoy,_ and _see,_ to start your descriptions.

Place/Activity 1

_____

_____

_____

_____

Place/Activity 2

_____

_____

_____

_____

Place/Activity 3

_____

_____

_____

_____

2. *Find photographs, pictures from magazines, or other illustrations of the things in your brochure.*

3. *Choose a title for the front of the brochure.*

_____

_____

Match Your Writing and Your Audience

Always keep in mind the people who will be reading your writing. They are your *audience*.

1. *Answer the following questions.*

   a. Who is the audience for a travel brochure? _____

   b. What do they need to know about the place in your travel brochure?

_____

_____

2. *Read your brochure again. Check to make sure that it gives enough information to your audience.*

EDITING TIP

When you write, think about your readers (the audience). What will they expect to read? What kind of information will they want? How much information do they need?

Editing Checklist

Check the Content

1. *Exchange your brochure with a classmate. After you read your classmate's brochure, answer these questions.*

   ❏ Are the descriptions clear?
   ❏ Do the headings help you understand the information?

Check the Details

2. *Read your brochure again. If necessary, revise what you wrote . Try to use different adjectives, nouns, and verbs. Then continue checking your own brochure. Use these questions.*

   ❏ Look at the headings and the descriptions you wrote. Did you use active verbs?
   ❏ Does every sentence begin with a capital letter and end with a period, a question mark, or an exclamation point?

3. *Make your corrections. Arrange the photos and your writing into a brochure.*

Vocabulary Log

What words or phrases would you like to remember from this chapter? Write five to ten items in your notebook. Examples are on page 10.

Grammar and Punctuation Review

Look over your writing from this chapter. What changes did you need to make in grammar and punctuation? Write them in your notebook. Review them before the next writing assignment.

Class Activity   Travel Display

Make a display of all the travel brochures the class made.

1 Look at all of the brochures. How can you display them—in a poster? In a packet? On a bulletin board?

2 Is there a way to group some brochures together? Think of ways to categorize them—for example, by area of the world (*Visit the Mediterranean!*), by type of activity (*Sunny Places or Ski Destinations*), or by type of travel (*Romantic Getaways, Adventure Travel, Great Trips for Families*).

3 Find a place to display your work.

Living Spaces ③

What type of living space do you need? How do you feel about your living space? This unit looks at living spaces—their appearance, their design, and problems people sometimes have with them.

These are some of the activities you will do in this unit:

- Use vocabulary to describe spaces
- Read descriptions of rooms and houses in different cultures
- Describe an important room in your culture
- Survey your classmates about their ideal living spaces
- Create a chart to report your survey results
- Read letters about a student center
- Write a letter of complaint
- Read a brochure about tenant's rights

Chapter 8

Interior Design

Starting Point

How is your house or room decorated? People's living spaces can be decorated in many different styles. This chapter gives you practice working with vocabulary to describe living spaces.

Kitchen Details

For many people in the United States, the kitchen is the center of their living space.

1. *Look at the room in the photograph. Now read the list of adjectives. Circle the words that you think of when you look at this room. Add some words of your own.*

warm	large	small	typical	practical
unusual	crowded	spacious	cluttered	empty
comfortable	peaceful	friendly	full	_____
strange	formal	informal	huge	_____
homey	efficient	traditional	modern	_____

2. *Is the room on page 65 similar to or different from a typical kitchen in your culture? Discuss your ideas with a classmate.*

Reading

Descriptions of Rooms

People have different ideas about the design of the space inside rooms. The look of this space is called its *interior design*.

1. *Read the descriptions of rooms below and on page 67. Match the rooms with the pictures. Write the correct letters next to the pictures.*

a. My family's house has a large room for entertaining visitors. It has a high ceiling, and it is very wide and open. There is not much furniture in it, just some comfortable, low couches along the walls and some small, low tables for coffee. There is a beautiful, soft rug on the floor. We enjoy sitting in this room.

b. My favorite room has a low table in the center. The table is called a *kotatsu,* a Japanese foot warmer. There is a heater under it. In cold weather, we sit around the table with our feet near the heat. A blanket covers the table and our legs so that we are warm. This is not the only furniture in the room, though. There is also a big chest and a book case on one side of the room.

c. Our family room has soft couches with a lot of pillows on them. The couches are next to each other, at a right angle, in a corner. They face the television set. Along one wall, we have bookshelves with lots of books, pictures, and electronic equipment. In another corner of the room, there is a piano. We spend a lot of time in this room!

d. My grandparents live in a traditional wood house with lots of windows. The living room area is raised. There is one small, low table and two or three triangle-shaped pillows for leaning on. The decorations are very beautiful. I would like to have a house like this someday.

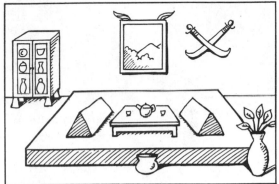

2. *Discuss these questions with a classmate.*

    a. Which room in exercise 1 seems most familiar to you? Which would you be most comfortable in?

    b. Which room is the most different from a room in your house? Why?

3. *Go back to the descriptions in exercise 1. Make a list of all the words that name things in rooms.*

_____ _____ _____ _____

_____ _____ _____ _____

_____ _____ _____ _____

_____ _____ _____ _____

_____ _____ _____ _____

_____ _____ _____ _____

Targeting

Spatial Prepositions

Descriptions of rooms often include words that tell about location. These words are called **spatial prepositions.**

A **preposition** is a word that is used before a noun or pronoun to show relationship. Some prepositions are used in phrases. Here are some common spatial prepositions.

above	facing	on
against	far from	on the left
along	in	on the right
around	in back of	on top of
behind	near	under
beside	next to	with

Look at the illustration. Then complete the sentences on the next page with prepositions from the list above. There may be more than one correct answer for some items.

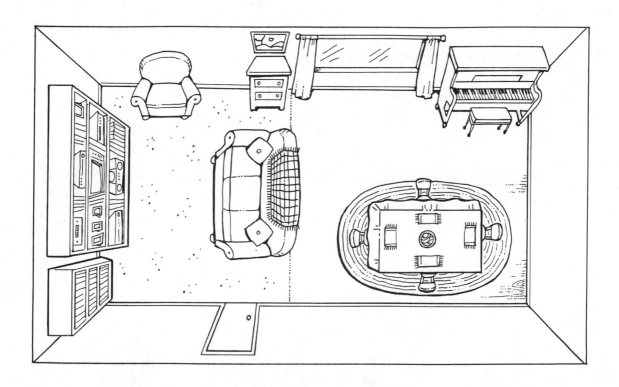

1. There is a piano _____*near*_____ the window.

2. The bookcase is _____ the wall.

3. A table _____ four chairs is on one side of the room.

4. There is a rug _____ the table.

5. A couch is _____ the television.

6. _____ the couch is a blanket and two pillows.

7. The chest is _____ the window.

8. An entertainment center _____ a television set and CD player is along one wall.

9. A telephone is on the wall _____ the table.

10. The chest is _____ the painting.

....

When you describe a room, you need to think of all the details. These exercises can help you picture the kinds of details to include. The design of rooms can affect the way we feel. Sometimes we feel comfortable in a room because of the way it looks. Sometimes, though, a room's size, design, or decor (*Interior decoration*) may make us feel very uncomfortable.

1. *Read the pairs of descriptions below. Can you picture the room? Which description in each pair gives better details? Put a check on the line. Then compare your answers with a classmate's answers.*

   a. _____ At night I study in my bedroom at home. I share this room with my brother, so it is very crowded. We have a table in the middle of the room. We study at this table.

   _____ At night I study in my bedroom at home. I share this room with my brother, so it is very crowded. We have two single beds and a dresser along the sides of the room. In the middle of the room, there is a table. We study at this table, and it is always full of papers and books. It is usually very messy.

Writing

Preparing to Write: Picturing the Details

(ANSWER KEY)

b. _____ My favorite room is our living room. It is not really beautiful, but it is very comfortable, with a large couch and a soft chair. We spend a lot of time here, watching TV or talking. When I think of my home, this is the room I picture.

_____ My favorite room is our living room. It is very comfortable. The room is full of beautiful things. We spend a lot of time here with family and friends.

2. *Work with a partner. Discuss the room you are in.*

a. Look at the room you are in now. Describe the room to your partner. If you need help, use these phrases to begin your description.

This room is . . .	It has . . .
There is/are . . .	On the left/right . . .
In the center . . .	Along the sides . . .

b. Do you like the room? Why or why not?

I like/don't like this room because . . .

3. *Student A: Describe a room that you like (in a home or in a public building) to your partner. Use some of these expressions. Student B: Draw a diagram of the room's layout on a piece of paper.*

What room is this?	There is/are . . .
This room has . . .	On the left/right . . .
In the center . . .	Along the sides . . .

Writing a Description of a Room

Write a description of an important room in your family's home or in your culture. Use words from this chapter, including spatial prepositions.

1. *Study these rules about subject and verb agreement.*

**Editing for
Subject-Verb
Agreement**

Rules	Examples
Every sentence has a **subject** and a **verb.**	The **room is** large. subject verb
The subject and verb need to **agree.** Both must be either singular or plural. Be careful with the third person singular (*he, she, it*).	I have a house in the city The house **has** five rooms. third person singular
If a list follows *there is/are* and starts with a *singular* noun, the verb is singular. If it starts with a *plural* noun, the verb is plural.	There **is** a living room, a kitchen, and two bedrooms in the apartment. There **are** three chairs and a couch in the room.
Note: When there are more than two items in a list, use commas to separate them.	The kitchen and dining room are connected. The kitchen, dining room, and living room are all connected.

2. *Are the verbs correct here? Put a check (✓) in front of the correct sentence(s).*

a. _____ My house have two floors and an attic.

b. _____ My apartment has three small rooms.

c. _____ The main rooms of my house is large.

d. _____ There are a living room, a dining room, and a kitchen on that floor.

e. _____ There are three closets, a bathroom, and a toilet.

3. *Is the punctuation correct here? Put a check (✓) in front of the correct sentences.*

a. _____ There is a bedroom, and a bathroom upstairs.

b. _____ There is a bathroom and three closets along the hallway.

c. _____ There are three closets, a bathroom, and a toilet.

d. _____ My house has four main rooms: a living room, a dining room a kitchen and a bedroom.

e. _____ The dining room, and living room are next to one another.

4. *Complete the sentences with one of the verb choices below each blank.*

Bathrooms in Japan (*a*) _____are_____ very different from
(is, are)
bathrooms in the United States. In bathrooms in the United States,

there (*b*) _____ a sink, a toilet, and a bathtub. Sometimes
(is, are)
the toilet is right next to the bathtub or shower.

In Japan, toilets (*c*) _____ always separate from the bathing
(is, are)
area. There (*d*) _____ usually only a toilet and a sink in the
(is, are)
room. People (*e*) _____ careful about germs in the toilet
(is, are)

area. A separate pair of slippers (*f*) _____ worn only in the
(is, are)
toilet. Because old houses sometimes (*g*) _____ not have
(does, do)
much heat in the winter, sometimes the toilet seat (*h*) _____
(has, have)
a heating element in it. This is very nice!

Bathrooms in Japan usually (*i*) _____ a tile floor and a
(has, have)
deep bathtub. (*j*) _____ a drain in the floor of the bathroom.
(Have, There is)
This drain is necessary because people (*k*) _____ and
(washes, wash)
(*l*) _____ themselves before they (*m*) _____ into the
(rinses, rinse)   (gets, get)
bathtub. Because people (*n*) _____ clean when they (*o*) _____
(is, are)   (takes, take)
a bath, more than one person (*p*) _____ able to use the
(is, are)
same bathwater. The bathwater is very hot, and it is very

pleasant to sit and soak in the tub. If there (*q*) _____ older
(is, are)
people in the family, they get to use the bath first.

When a Japanese person (*r*) _____ to the United States,
(goes, go)
he or she (*s*) _____ the Japanese bath a lot!
(misses, miss)

5. *Add correct punctuation to these sentences, if needed. Some*
   sentences are correct.

   a. My bedroom has a bookshelf, a bed, and a dresser.
   b. In the living room there is only one small table a rug and a
      few pillows.
   c. The apartment has two phone jacks a cable TV hook-up and
      space for a microwave.
   d. A painting two photographs and two swords hang on the
      walls.
   e. I have a TV a video and a CD player.
   f. In the summer there is a flowered mat of bamboo.
   g. There is almost always a fireplace in houses in the United
      States.

Editing Checklist

Check the Content

1. *Exchange your description from page 70 with a classmate. After you read your classmate's description, answer these questions.*

   ❏ Is there enough information in the description?
   ❏ Can you picture the room? Can you picture the details?

Check the Details

2. *Read your description again. If necessary, revise what you wrote. Add more information and more details. Then continue checking your own writing. Use these questions.*

   ❏ Check the spatial prepositions. Do they show correct location?
   ❏ Does each singular subject have a singular verb form? Does each plural subject have a plural verb form?
   ❏ Did you begin each sentence with a capital letter and end it with a period, a question mark, or an exclamation point?
   ❏ Are there any lists? Did you use commas to separate the items?

3. *Correct your description from exercise 1. Then rewrite it.*

Vocabulary Log

What words or phrases would you like to remember from this chapter? Write five to ten items in your notebook. Examples are on page 10.

Grammar and Punctuation Review

Look over your writing from this chapter. What changes did you need to make in grammar and punctuation? Write them in your notebook. Review them before the next writing assignment.

Class Activity   Where Am I?

1 Think of (or go to) a room your classmates know.

2 Write a description of this room.

3 Read your description to your classmates. Can they guess which room it is?

Chapter 9

House Layout

Houses in different cultures have different designs. In this chapter you will read about some of these differences, survey your class-mates, and create a chart to show the survey results.

Starting Point

Houses in Different Cultures

Balinese
Mediterranean
Swiss
North American
Southeast Asian

A world with only one style of house would certainly be boring! People build houses to fit the culture, the climate, and sometimes the land around the house.

1. *Match the houses in the photos with the name of the style. Write the style on the line.*

_____

_____

Balinese

2. _Look at the photos of houses again and answer the questions._

    a. Find two houses that are similar. Which houses are they?
    How are they similar?

    _____

    _____

    b. Find two houses that are different. Which houses are they?
    How are they different?

    _____

    _____

Reading

International Design in Houses

Building styles are more similar around the world nowadays, but there are still a lot of differences in the design of houses.

1. *Read the following selection.*

International Design in Houses

[1] McDonald's golden arches and Baskin and Robbins' 31 flavors—you can often find the same fast-food restaurants in different countries. High-rise apartment buildings also often look the same wherever you go. With countries becoming so similar, you might expect us all to live in similar living spaces. In fact, there are still many differences in houses from place to place.

[2] The layout of a typical house depends on the region. In Korea, China, and parts of Latin America, for example, houses are often built around courtyards. Rooms open onto or have a view of this common outdoor space. "Euro-American" houses, on the other hand, usually have rooms opening onto an interior hallway.

[3] In the South Pacific, where the weather is warm, families often live in groups of open-air buildings. In the Turkish countryside, there is often a patio covered with grape vines. This *cardak* gives the family a cool place to spend time in the summer. In cold areas of the United States and Canada, many houses have "mud rooms," where people leave their boots and heavy coats.

[4] Some differences in the layout of houses show the customs of an area. In some Muslim countries, houses have separate areas for males and females. In Japan, the front entrance often is very practical. People keep footwear on shelves there because they do not wear outdoor shoes in the house. Many homes around the world have special areas related to tradition or religion. For example, in many Buddhist homes, a small area is set up to remember gods or ancestors.

[5] House design changes as lifestyles change. In the United States, many houses built after 1950 had "family rooms," or informal living areas, in them. These family rooms were often in basements or far away from the formal living areas. In newer houses, this family room is often combined with the kitchen and eating area. It is sometimes called a "great room." Although many houses in the United States still have formal living and dining rooms, in time the "great room" may replace these more formal areas completely.

[6] The differences in design from place to place are very interesting. They reflect differences in culture, lifestyles, and tradition, as well as differences in the weather.

After you read something, you can remember the information by **taking notes**. Putting your notes in a chart helps you to organize the information.

2. *Complete the chart with information from the reading. A couple of boxes are completed for you.*

DIFFERENCES IN LAYOUT OF HOUSES IN DIFFERENT REGIONS		
Layout	Country/Region	Description
		an open-air dwelling
	Turkey	

Layout	Country/Region	Description

3. *Work with a partner or small group. Look at the rooms in the chart in exercise 2. Discuss these questions.*

a. Do these house designs tell us anything about the culture? What is an example of a design related to a value such as cleanliness, privacy, or formality?

b. What is an example of a design related to a religious custom?

c. Can you think of any examples of interesting house designs from your own experience?

Reflect on Reading

The chart in exercise 2 contains your notes from the reading "International Design in Houses." **Taking notes in a chart** can help you to understand information. A chart also helps you if you need to look at your notes. Do you like to use charts and lists when you take notes? Why or why not? Discuss with a partner.

Quickwriting: The Perfect Place to Live

What is your idea of the perfect place to live? In your notebook, write for five to ten minutes about this ideal place. It doesn't have to be a house. Use your imagination!

Writing

Preparing to Write Part 1: Conducting a Survey

In this section, the information you collect about people and their living spaces will be the data for a chart. Charting is helpful both as a way to take notes from your reading and as a way to show information when you write, especially if you are writing in business or technical situations.

1. *Ask your classmates these questions about their ideal houses. On a separate sheet, record their answers.*

   The person I talked to is ☐ male   ☐ female

   from _____ (country)

   from ☐ a city

   ☐ a suburb

   ☐ a rural area

   a. Would you prefer to live in ☐ a house or ☐ an apartment?

   b. Would you prefer to live in ☐ the city, ☐ the suburbs, or ☐ the country?

   c. Is it ☐ a house, ☐ an apartment, or ☐ a collection of smaller buildings?

   d. If you have a family with two parents and five children (three boys and two girls), how many bedrooms do you need?

   _____

   e. Is the kitchen ☐ a central place for the family or is it ☐ only for the person preparing meals?

   f. Is the living room ☐ just for entertaining guests or is it ☐ an informal room for the family?

2. *Write a few of your own questions. Ask your classmates the questions and record their answers.*

   _____

   _____

   _____

   _____

   _____

Charts can help show information when you write or make reports. In this exercise, you will plan a chart to show the results of your survey.

1. *Choose a title for your chart. Here are some possibilities:*

   Design Preferences   Typical Homes

   Preferences about _____ Homes _____
                                (your idea)

   Your chart's title: _____

2. *Choose categories to put at the top of the chart. Here are some possibilities:*
   Male, Female   Country A, Country B, Country C
   Region A, Region B

   Your chart's categories:

   _____   _____

   _____   _____

   _____   _____

   _____   _____

   _____   _____

3. *Decide how to show the different answers from your survey. Do not use complete sentences. Try to use short phrases or nouns. You don't have to include everything you find out in the survey! Here are some possibilities:*

	Men	Women
Prefer Apartments	79%	50%

	Korea	Canada
Courtyard		✓

   How will you show the information in your chart—in percentages, numbers, or with yes/no?

   _____

4. Write a short introduction to your chart. You may want to give some information about the group you surveyed (nationalities/gender/number of people) and the general topic of the survey or any surprising results.

_____

_____

_____

Writing Survey Results in a Chart

Create your own chart to show your survey results. If you need help, work with a partner or a small group. Then share your chart with the class.

_____
(title)

_____
(introduction)
_____

_____

Editing Checklist

Check the Content

1. *Exchange your chart with a classmate. After you look at your classmate's chart, answer these questions.*

   ❏ Does the introduction help you understand the information in the chart?
   ❏ Is the chart complete and easy to read?

Check the Details

2. *Look at your chart again. If necessary, revise your chart. Try to show the information more clearly. Use different categories, if necessary. Change some information to short phrases or nouns. Then continue checking your own writing. Ask these questions.*

   ❏ Is it difficult to show all the information in the same way (percentages, numbers)?
   ❏ If so, did you make a different section or write the information in a paragraph instead of in the chart?

3. *Make your corrections. Rewrite your chart if necessary.*

Vocabulary Log

What words or phrases would you like to remember from this chapter? Write five to ten items in your notebook. Examples are on page 10.

Grammar and Punctuation Review

Look over your writing from this chapter. What changes did you need to make in grammar and punctuation? Write them in your notebook. Review them before the next writing assignment.

Chapter 10

A Home Away from Home

People often spend more time away from home than at home. Students sometimes get tired of going from class to class with "no place to call home" at school. In this chapter, you will read students' letters about a place to spend free time and write about your own situation.

Starting Point

Needs Analysis

Do you need a "home away from home" at your school?

Discuss these questions with a partner or a small group.

1. Where do you spend time during breaks or in between classes?
2. Is this place satisfactory? Are you happy with this situation?

Reading

Student Letters

On pages 87–88, there are two letters about a place for students to spend their free time. Some ideas are the same in two letters, and some are different.

> **READING TIP**
>
> When you **compare** ideas, look for what is the same and what is different.

1. *Students at a large community college in Oklahoma wanted the president to make some changes for them. Read the letters to the president from two groups of students.*

February 23, 1998

Simon Jefferson
President
City Community College
Tulsa, OK 74103

Dear President Jefferson:

The Student Association would like to ask you to consider building an addition to the cafeteria. This would benefit all students because
• We sometimes have to wait hours between classes.
• We cannot study in the cafeteria. It's too noisy and crowded.
• We need lockers for our belongings.

We are willing to help pay for this addition with money from the student activities fund.

We hope that you will consider our request. Thank you.

Sincerely,

Walter Schmidt   Danielle LeDuc   Jamal Al-Aziz

Student Association Members

Letter B

February 23, 1998

Simon Jefferson
President
City Community College
Tulsa, OK 74103

Dear President Jefferson:

As students here at the City Community College, we often have a lot of
time between classes. We would like to study in this free time. However,
the cafeteria is crowded and noisy. The library does not have enough tables.
There is really no place to study.

We hope that you will ask the city for money to build a student center with
• a study area with comfortable chairs as well as regular
  tables and chairs
• lockers for our belongings
• a covered area outside for smokers
• a coffee shop
• a computer lab

We would also like to suggest a name for the center: the Jefferson Building.

Thank you for considering our proposal.

Sincerely,

Walter Schmidt   *Danielle Le Duc*   *Jamal Al-Aziz*

2. *Find words in the students' letters with the same meaning as the*
words in the list.

a. think about　　　　　　　　　　_____

b. be good for　　　　　　　　　　_____

c. full of people　　　　　　　　　_____

d. secure places to store things　_____

e. things you own   _____

f. collection of money   _____

g. with a roof   _____

3. *To complete these sentences about the students' letters, circle the best word or words. Try not to look at the letters. More than one answer may be possible for some items.*

ANSWER KEY

   a. The students wanted a place to _____ .
       study   rest

   b. They wrote a letter to _____ .
       the Student Association   the college president

   c. Each letter had _____ plan.
       the same   a different

   d. In my opinion, the president will probably say _____ to the
                                        (yes / no)

       request in letter A and _____ to the request in letter B.
                          (yes / no)

4. **Analyzing the organization** *of a reading is an important reading skill. Both letters are well-written, but they are organized differently. Read the letters again and compare the differences.*

ANSWER KEY

   a. Which reasons do the students give in letter A? In letter B? Write *A* and/or *B* on the lines.

       a lot of time between classes   _____   _____

       problems with studying in the cafeteria   _____   _____

       problems with the library   _____   _____

       need for a place to keep personal things   _____   _____

   b. What does the proposal in letter A *not* include? Write a check next to the items.

       _____ lockers   _____ a study area

       _____ a smoking area   _____ a computer lab

       _____ a coffee shop

c. Both letter A and letter B use **bulleted lists** (lists after a • mark). What information is in each list? Write *A* or *B* on the lines.

_____ their reasons   _____ their ideas

Quickwriting: Reacting with Your Ideas

Does your school or college have a place for students to relax or study? If it does, could it be better? If it doesn't, do you think the school needs one? In your notebook, write for five or ten minutes about these questions.

Vocabulary Log

What words or phrases would you like to remember from this chapter? Write five to ten items in your notebook. Examples are on page 10.

Chapter 11

Housing Problems

Sometimes people have problems with their living spaces. In this chapter you will learn the vocabulary to explain about problems and write a letter of complaint.

Starting Point

In any kind of living space, you can experience problems.

Identifying Problems

1. *Discuss these questions with a partner or a small group.*

a. Do you, your family, or people in your class rent an apartment or a house?

_____

_____

_____

b. Who owns it—a company or one person (a *landlord*)?

_____

_____

_____

c. Do you ever have problems with the company or your landlord? List some possible problems. The first suggestion is made for you.

The landlord raises the rent.

_____

_____

_____

_____

_____

d. Look at the picture of the apartment building below. What kinds of problems does this building have? Write them here.

The roof leaks. (There is a leak in the . . .)

_____

_____

_____

_____

e. Have you ever had any problems like these?

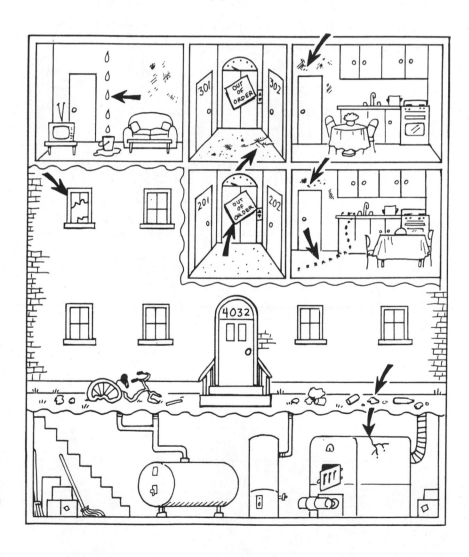

Reading

Your Rights as a Tenant

People who live in apartment buildings are called tenants. In most large cities, tenants can get help if their landlord doesn't take care of the apartment. This reading gives some information from a brochure published in New York State. The information may not apply to every city in every state, but it is typical of tenants' rights information.

1. *Read the following selection.*

Your Rights as a Tenant

YOUR RIGHTS AS A TENANT

- *How often must my landlord paint my apartment?*

Your landlord must paint your apartment once every three years. No payment for the paint or the work is required from the tenant.

- *What about heat and hot water?*

During the heating season (October 1 through May 31) your landlord must provide heat as follows: During the day (6 a.m. to 10 p.m.), if the temperature outside is below 55 degrees (fahrenheit), your apartment must be at least 68 degrees. At night (10 p.m. to 6 a.m.), if the temperature is below 40 degrees, your apartment must be at least 55 degrees. Your landlord must supply hot water at a constant minimum temperature of 120 degrees.

- *What services must my landlord provide?*

You have the right to a safe, well-maintained, livable apartment. You also have the right to hold tenants' meetings in your building and make complaints about any lack of services.

Your landlord must
- list a phone number in the building where the owner or agent can be reached at all times.
- provide regular extermination services, if needed, to control bugs.
- provide a place for garbage disposal
- keep public areas (inside and out) clean and free of vermin such as cockroaches or rats.
- provide janitorial services to keep the building clean.
- keep the building in good repair. In apartments this means the walls, ceilings, floors, windows, plumbing, heating, light fixtures, doors, lock(s) on the outer door of each apartment, lighting in building public areas, peepholes on entrance doors, and main building door locks.
- follow all safety and fire code regulations.

- *What if I don't receive proper services or repairs?*

If you have a problem, first speak to your landlord. If your landlord does not respond to your complaint, write to your landlord by certified mail. Keep copies of your correspondence or a record of your conversations. If your landlord does not act in a reasonable period of time, see if there is a housing commission in your area. You can file a complaint there about problems in your apartment, such as no hot water, a leaking roof, or cockroaches.

There are two other possibilities, but it is a good idea to ask a lawyer about them first. One is to stop paying your rent until the landlord makes repairs or provides services. Another is to make the repairs yourself and deduct the cost from your rent.

READING TIP

This reading contains frequently asked questions about tenants' rights. When you reread to find information, look at the question. Think about whether the answer has the information you need.

2. *Match the definitions on the right with the words in **boldface** from the reading. Write the correct letter on the line.*

a. no **payment** from the tenant   _____ answer

b. at a constant **minimum** tempera-   _____ absence of
ture of 120 degrees

c. a safe, well-maintained, **livable**   _____ controlling prob-
apartment   lems with bugs

d. make complaints about **lack** of   _____ pipes and fixtures
services   of water and
                                                         sewage in a
                                                         building

e. provide regular **extermination**   _____ take out, subtract
services if needed

f. keep public areas (inside and out)   _____ money paid
clean and free of **vermin**

g. provide **janitorial** services   _____ lowest possible

h. **plumbing,** heating   _____ pests such as cock-
                                                         roaches or rats

i. **adequate** lighting   _____ enough, satisfactory

j. does not **respond to** your   _____ cleaning
complaint

k. **deduct** the cost from your rent   _____ possible to live in

3. *Imagine that you live in the apartment building pictured on page 92. According to "Your Rights as a Tenant," does the landlord have to fix all the problems in your building? Underline any information about your problems.*

4. *What can you infer from the reading? Which problems in the illustration are not mentioned directly? Is it possible that the landlord may still be required to fix them? Discuss with a partner.*

5. *The brochure "Your Rights as a Tenant" explains how to get the landlord to fix problems. Read the brochure again. Now, make a list of the steps you should follow if you have a problem with your landlord.*

_____

_____

_____

_____

_____

_____

_____

Reflect on Reading

The brochure titled "Your Rights as a Tenant" uses the format of **frequently asked questions**. For which of the following kinds of information would this format also be useful? Discuss with a partner.

A short story   Information in a doctor's office about an illness   Directions for cooking a frozen pizza

Targeting

Word Forms

When you learn new words, it helps to think about their related forms.

1. *Complete this chart with words from "Your Rights as a Tenant" on page 93. Write the verb or the noun form of the word given.*

ANSWER KEY

Noun	Verb
payment	pay
make a _____	complain about
_____	own
_____	build
response	_____ to
deduction	_____

2. *Complete the sentences with words from the chart in exercise 1.*

a. Our landlord did not _____ to our letter, so I am calling a lawyer.

b. Our _____ needs repairs to the following immediately: the plumbing on the second floor, the fire escape, and the lock on the front door.

c. If you do not make these repairs, we will hire someone to do the work and _____ the cost of the repairs from our rent.

d. The _____ of our building lives here, too, so she is very good about making repairs.

e. A security deposit is an additional _____ that most land-lords require when you rent an apartment. If there is no damage to the apartment, you will get the deposit back when you move out.

f. We complained to the landlord, but he didn't do anything. We are going to make a _____ to the housing commission.

WRITING TIP

Usually, a formal letter has the sender's address at the top. The letter on page 97 doesn't because a group of people are writing. Their address is in the first line. In a formal letter, always include your address.

Writing

Preparing to Write: Including Details

Sometime you may need to write a letter of complaint to your landlord about the problems in your living space. The letter on page 97 gives you practice in writing the important details clearly and directly.

Complete this letter to the landlord of the building pictured on page 92. Describe the problems in this apartment building.

September 25, 1998

Kent Smith
City Buildings
2 Center Plaza
Philadelphia, PA 19109

Dear Mr. Smith:

We live at 4032 Walnut Street. Your company recently bought our apartment building. This building needs immediate attention to the following problems:

- There is a leak _____ .
- Apartment 201 needs _____ .
- The _____ doesn't work.
- The _____ doesn't work.
- There _____ in the kitchen of Apartment 202.
- A window on the second floor_____ .
- The yard _____ .
- _____ new paint.

These conditions make this building dangerous and unlivable. We called you many times, and you have not done anything about them. If you do not fix these problems within one month, we will get a lawyer to help us take the necessary steps to make the building safe and livable.

Sincerely,

(your signature under your printed name)
Tenants' Association Member

Writing a Letter of Complaint

Here is your chance to write about some real problems in your living space.

Write a letter to your landlord. Describe the problem(s) in your building or apartment. Use real information or make something up.

Be sure your letter is in business letter format. If you need help with vocabulary, go back to the Starting Point exercises and the practice letter of complaint you wrote in this chapter.

> A formal letter follows **business letter format.** The example on page 97 shows one example of business letter format. For another example of business letter format, see pages 195–196 in Reference.

Editing and Rewriting

Editing Checklist

Check the Content

1. *Exchange your letter of complaint with a classmate. After you read your classmate's letter, answer these questions.*

   ❏ Is there enough information in the letter?
   ❏ Does the writer state the problems clearly and directly?

Check the Details

2. *Now, reread your letter of complaint. If necessary, revise what you wrote. Add more information and more details. Then continue checking your own writing. Use these questions.*

   ❏ Does each singular subject have a singular verb form? Does each plural subject have a plural verb form?
   ❏ Are there any lists in sentences? Did you use commas to separate the items?
   ❏ Are the city, country, and zip code correct?
   ❏ Did you write the date in the order of month/day/year?

3. *Make your corrections. Rewrite your letter.*

Vocabulary Log

What words or phrases would you like to remember from this chapter? Write five to ten items in your notebook. Examples are on page 10.

Grammar and Punctuation Review

Look over your writing from this chapter. What changes did you need to make in grammar and punctuation? Write them in your notebook. Review them before the next writing assignment.

The E-mail Revolution

Have you ever used e-mail? Electronic mail, or "e-mail," is one of the newest and fastest forms of communication. In this section, you will read and write about e-mail in both business and personal uses.

These are some of the activities you will do in this unit:

- Read about traveling by computer
- Read rules about the proper use of e-mail
- Read and write e-mail messages
- Read about problems with e-mail in the workplace
- Write a policy for e-mail use at work

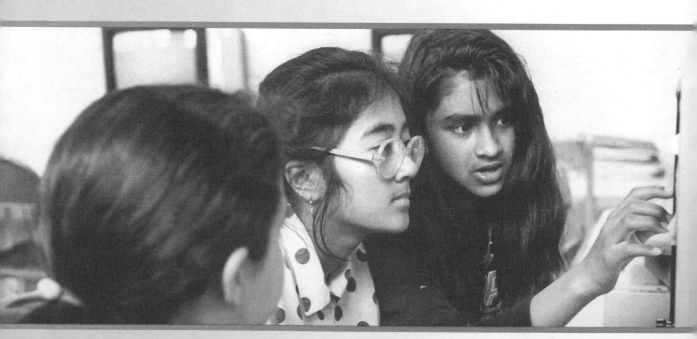

E-mail allows us to travel around the world, without leaving home, work, or school. In this chapter you will read an article about using computers to travel electronically and you will write about your own computer experience.

Traveling by Computers

Starting Point

E-mail is short for "electronic mail." This section contains some other computer vocabulary for you to identify.

Look at this illustration. Choose appropriate words to put in the blanks in the sentences.

Getting to Know E-mail

1. Someone on a ___*computer*___ in Korea can "talk" to someone in Syria by e-mail.

2. We use computers to communicate with people by sending _____ over the Internet.

3. You need four things to send messages: a computer, _____, a modem, and a telephone line.

4. A _____ connects the communications software to the telephone line.

5. Millions of interconnected computers around the world make up _____.

Reading

Traveling by Computer

READING TIP

You don't always need to look up new words in a dictionary. **Context clues** can help you guess the meanings of unfamiliar words.

Computers are rapidly changing our lives and opening doors to the rest of the world. This reading describes the revolutionary changes created by electronic mail.

1. *Read the following selection.*

Traveling by Computer

[1] Electronic mail, or "e-mail," is causing a revolution in our lives just as the telephone did. It is changing the way we communicate with one another. This speedy, informal means of communication is becoming more and more popular among all age groups around the world. To use it, all you need is a computer, communications software, a modem, and a phone line. Once you have an e-mail address, you can "talk" to people all over the world. Millions of people have e-mail addresses.

[2] Why is e-mail becoming more popular than regular, or "snail," mail? First of all, it's fast. You can send your message in seconds instead of days. In addition, e-mail is cheaper than regular mail. You are using your telephone line, but the cost is much lower than the cost of regular calls on your telephone bill. E-mail is also very convenient. It is easy to use because you and the other person don't have to be on the line at the same time. You can write your message when you have time. The other person can read it when he or she has time. You can start to write a message, save it, and continue it later. You can print messages and save them. E-mail is also good for the environment: It uses no trees, no paper, and no gasoline!

[3] Finally, your e-mail account is your doorway to the Internet, a "superhighway" of millions of interconnected computers. You can find books, journals, information, computer software, and even

whole libraries from around the world there. You can get the current news, sports results, and weather information. You can also "meet" people and discuss topics you're interested in. Another attraction is that everyone is equal on e-mail. You can't see how people look or how much money they have. The written word is popular again. Your own words and ideas are important. With your e-mail account, you will become a traveler in a world without time zones or borders.

2. *Match these words with their definitions. Write the letters on the lines.*

ANSWER KEY

   a. e-mail   _____ paper mail sent through the post office

   b. "snail" mail   _____ easy to use

   c. modem   _____ a link between your computer and telephone lines

   d. convenient   _____ a network of computers around the world

   e. the Internet   _a_ mail sent and received through a

3. *List six advantages of e-mail. The first one is done for you.*

ANSWER KEY

   a. _It's fast_____.

   b. _____.

   c. _____.

   d. _____.

   e. _____.

   f. _____.

4. Sometimes words are in quotation marks (" ") because their meanings are different from their usual meanings. **Scan** the reading to find the words in quotation marks that match these meanings. Write the words in the blanks.

   a. _____ begin communication through e-mail messages with someone you don't know

   b. _____ send and receive written messages on the computer

   c. _____ very slow

   d. _____ all of the interconnected computers that make up the Internet

5. Discuss these questions with a classmate.

   a. Do you use a computer?
   b. If so, are you comfortable using a computer?
   c. Do you use e-mail?
   d. Do you use the Internet?
   e. Do you think computers are changing people's lives too much and too fast?

Quickwriting: Computer Experience

How much experience do you have with computers? With e-mail? With the Internet? How do you feel about using this technology? In your notebook, write for five to ten minutes about how comfortable you are with computers.

Vocabulary Log

What words or phrases would you like to remember from this chapter? Write five to ten items in your notebook. Examples are on page 10.

Chapter 13

Using E-mail

Have you ever used e-mail? In this chapter you will learn about the parts of an e-mail message and the rules of using e-mail. Then you'll write an e-mail message.

....

This section will help you understand the organization of typical e-mail messages.

1. *Read the parts of an e-mail message in the list. Then read the e-mail message below. Write the letters of the correct words in the list in the circles on the e-mail message.*

_____ **a.** sender

_____ **b.** date and time of the message

_____ **c.** receiver

_____ **d.** sender's e-mail address

_____ **e.** receiver's e-mail address

_____ **f.** subject of message

_____ **g.** message

The Parts of an E-mail Message

READING TIP FOR E-MAIL

The date and time in an e-mail message are put in by the computer. The time shows the hour, minute, and second when the e-mail message was sent.

⃝Date: Mon, 22 Nov 1998 06:09:38
⃝From: Greta Borg <gborg@su.se> ⃝
⃝To: Sam Hujak <shujak@u.washington.edu> ⃝
⃝Subject: Student List

Dear Sam:

Hi! Sorry I didn't answer your message earlier. I was on vacation for a week. I hope you did well on your exams!

I'm thinking about studying in Canada next year, and I'd like to find out what experiences other people have had. Didn't you tell me about an e-mail discussion group for students? Could you tell me how to participate in it?

Thanks!
Greta

2. *On the lines, write **T** if the sentence is true and **F** if it is false.*

a. _____ Greta sent this message at 9:38 a.m.

b. _____ Greta is replying to a message from Sam.

c. _____ Sam and Greta probably know each other from work.

d. _____ Greta is studying in Canada.

e. _____ Greta wants information from Sam about studying in Canada.

Reading

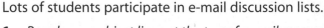

E-mail Messages

Lots of students participate in e-mail discussion lists.

1. *People use subject lines at the top of e-mail messages to give the message a title. Read the e-mail messages and then fill in the appropriate subject lines from this list.*

Living in Vancouver	Cold and Warm Places	Studying in Canada

Montreal   ✓ Discussion List

a.

Date: Fri, 2 Dec 1998 4:47:02
From: Sam Hujak <shujak@u.washington.edu>
To: Greta Borg <gborg@su.se>
Subject: ___Discussion List___

Hi, Greta!

Glad to hear from you. Where did you go on vacation?

To participate in the discussion list, go into the Newsgroups section of your e-mail program and type 'misc.education.language. english'. Then compose a message with this text in it:

    SUBSCRIBE MISC.EDUCATION.LANGUAGE.ENGLISH

You'll start to receive all the messages from this e-mail discussion group, and you can send your message to everyone on the list. I'm sure that a lot of the students on this list are in Canada.

Talk to you soon!
Sam

b.

Date: Sat, 3 Dec 1998 10:45:09
From: Greta Borg <gborg@su.se>
Newsgroups: misc.education.language.english
Subject: _____

Hi! I'm new to this list, and I'm thinking about studying in Canada next year. Do any of you live in Canada? Could you tell me about your experiences there? I'm thinking about studying in either Montreal or Vancouver.

Thank you,
Greta Borg

c.

Date: Sat, 3 Dec 1998 12:09:33
From: Francois DuPontois <francois@frl.physics.mcgill.ca>
To: Greta Borg <gborg@su.se>
Newsgroups: misc.education.language.english

Subject: _____

Greta:

I've been living in Montreal for six months, and I love it! I'm studying at McGill University. Montreal is a beautiful city, and there is a lot to do here. The only problem is the weather. It's cold! But you probably wouldn't mind as much as I did. I'm from Haiti, so it was a terrible adjustment. I didn't have any winter clothes.

I'd be happy to give you more information if you decide to come to Montreal.

Francois DuPontois

d.

Date: Sat, 3 Dec 1998 12:12:33
From: Tony Liu <tliu@troy.sfu.ca>
To: Greta Borg <gborg@su.se>
Newsgroups: misc.education.language.english
Subject: _____

YOU SHOULD DEFINITELY COME TO VANCOUVER. IT'S SO BEAUTIFUL, YOU WON'T BELIEVE IT, WITH MOUNTAINS AND WATER EVERYWHERE YOU LOOK. THERE ARE LOTS OF PLACES TO STUDY HERE. WHAT FIELD ARE YOU IN?

I DIDN'T HAVE ANY DIFFICULTIES HERE, BUT I MOVED HERE WITH MY FAMILY. IT MIGHT BE DIFFERENT FOR YOU. I THINK EVERYONE HERE IS VERY FRIENDLY THOUGH.

ONE THING TO CONSIDER IS THE COST OF LIVING. IT'S MORE EXPENSIVE HERE THAN EAST OF THE ROCKIES, BUT IT'S WORTH IT!

SEND ME A MESSAGE IF YOU WANT TO CHAT MORE.

TONY LIU

e.

Date: Sun, 4 Dec 1998 10:29:47
From: gmenotti@dbcc.cc.fl
To: Greta Borg <gborg@su.se>
Newsgroups: misc.education.language.english

_____

Subject:

Get serious, you guys! It's freezing cold in Montreal, and it rains all the time in Vancouver. Greta should come to someplace warm to study, like Florida! Studying here is like being on vacation. We can go to the beach almost every day. People like to party down here!

Being in another country is difficult sometimes, but I think it is an important experience. It makes me think about my life at home in a different way. I think I will always have a different perspective because I lived in another country.

Have to go -- another beach day!
Giovanni Menotti

2. *Through common practice, people who use e-mail have developed some rules regarding correct e-mail etiquette, or politeness. Read these rules.*

E-mail Rules

In any message:

1. Always give a subject in the subject line.
2. DO NOT TYPE IN ALL CAPS! Typing in all caps means you are angry or shouting.
3. Separate paragraphs with a blank line.
4. *Remember:* Even when you're writing a personal e-mail message, e-mail is not completely private. Think: What if someone else got this message by mistake?

3. *The messages on pages 106–108 break some of the rules of e-mail etiquette. What did the users do wrong? Apply the rules to the messages. For the e-mail messages, write the number of the broken rule on the line. There may be more than one broken rule in a message.*

Message A: _____

Message B: _____

Message C: _____

Message D: _____

Message E: _____

Reflect on Reading

If you understand what you read, you should be able to use the information in different situations. This is called **applying information.** You did this when you applied the rules from the reading in exercise 3. This skill involves **critical thinking**—analyzing information or situations. In which of these situations would you need to apply information from your reading? Discuss with a classmate.

    Reading the newspaper

    Reading the directions to set up your new computer

    Reading a recipe

4. *Greta wrote to a newsgroup related to English language studies. There are hundreds of newsgroups around the world. Their names usually consist of a major category word or abbreviation and then more specific details. Some of the codes are* alt *(alternative group),* rec *(recreational activities and hobbies),* sci *(science), and* soc *(society/culture).*

Match these newsgroup addresses to the appropriate messages. Write the address next to the letter at the top of the message.

croatia.newsgroup.discussion   alt.auto.toyota
alt.business.import-export   alt.sci.communications

a.

Subject: 88 Camry for Sale

88 Toyota Camry
under 90K miles
white inside and out
automatic
four door
excellent condition

must sell
$5000 or best offer

Please call Melinda at 306-482-6375.
Leave message.

b.

Subject: Communications Research Paper

Can you help? I have to do a research paper for my Communications 101 class. My problem is I need a topic. If you have any ideas, please e-mail me. I only have one month!

Thanks in advance for your help!

Marc Latterly

c.

Subject: Looking for South American Textile Importers

Our company has 20 years of experience making cotton and linen cloth. We'd like to do business with South American importers.

Interested parties contact:
Phuong Lee
Tel: 86-677-2297433
Fax: 86-677-2459395
E-mail: plee@asiacloth.net.cn

d.

Subject: Looking for a Croatian pen pal

I am a 24-year-old single female studying Slavic linguistics at the University of Illinois. I'd really like to write to someone in Croatia to learn more about the culture and the language.

Gloria Maravilla

Targeting

E-mail Addresses

E-mail addresses help us know who the user is and from where he or she is writing.

The first part of the address is the *login name*. It is sometimes limited to eight letters. Many people use their first and/or second initial and their last name. For example, Mary Brown's login is **mbrown.**

1. *Match these login names with the possible users. Write the letters of the possible users in the blanks next to the login name.*

Login Names

_____ _____   slacey

_____ _____   gborg

_____ _____   thiller

_____ _____   phowell

Possible Users

a.	Susan Lacey	**e.**	Peter Hill Owell
b.	Guy Borgian	**f.**	Greta Borg
c.	Ted Hiller	**g.**	Sheryl Lacey
d.	Tom Hiller	**h.**	Patty Howell

2. *Make an e-mail login name for yourself.* _____

> The second part of the e-mail address comes after the @ sign. This is the name of the company, school, or group, followed by a period or "dot" and a code for the type of organization. These are typical organization codes:
>
> .org   organization
> .com   commercial
> .edu   education (university or college)
> .gov   government

3. *What do you expect the following to have in their e-mail address as their organization type? Write the type code next to the correct name.*

a. _____ the University of New Mexico

b. _____ Disney Corporation

c. _____ the Red Cross

d. _____ the United States Postal Service

Some e-mail addresses also contain a country code.

ANSWER KEY

4. _Codes for six different countries are given below. Write the country code next to the correct country._

.ca   .ja   .uk   .se   .tw   .mx

a. _____ Canada   **d.** _____ Japan

b. _____ Taiwan   **e.** _____ Mexico

c. _____ the United Kingdom **f.** _____ Sweden

5. _Make a complete e-mail address for yourself._

_____

Writing

Preparing to Write: E-mail Subject Lines

Subject lines tell your reader quickly what a message contains. Sometimes you will have lots of messages, so the subject line helps you find a certain message without actually reading or even looking at the message.

Subject lines in e-mail are usually short, precise, specific phrases—not complete sentences.	Next Meeting Spring Break Trip Wednesday Plans

1. _Put a check (✓) in front of the best subject line._

____ I'd recommend Montreal.

____ Montreal's a good place.

____ Montreal

2. *Change these sentences to subject lines.*

    a. I need information about ESL programs.

    _____

    b. We have lots to do before the trip.

    _____

    c. This discussion list will help you.

    _____

    d. Is there a good school in Alberta, Canada?

    _____

    e. I got an angry e-mail message.

    _____

    f. Twenty million people are using e-mail.

    _____

Writing an E-mail Message

When you reply to an e-mail message, the *To, From,* and *Date* information is automatically provided. When you create a new message, you will need to provide the *To* name.

Write an e-mail message to Greta. Tell her where she should go in the world to study English. Give reasons for your choice.

EDITING TIP

Writers often forget to add the **-s** or **-es** ending when they are using the present tense form with *he, she,* or *it.* Always make one editing "pass" through your writing just to check for this error.

Editing Checklist

Check the Content

1. *Exchange your e-mail message with a classmate. After you read your classmate's message, answer these questions.*

   ❑ Did the writer explain why Greta should study there?
   ❑ Is there a subject line?
   ❑ Is the subject line a word or phrase rather than a complete sentence?
   ❑ Did the writer break any rules of e-mail etiquette?

Check the Details

2. *Now, reread your e-mail message. Keep in mind the questions in exercise 1. If necessary, revise what you wrote. Then continue checking your own writing. Use these questions.*

   ❑ Did you use the present tense to tell about habits, facts, and general truths?
   ❑ Is there an **-s** or **-es** ending for third person singular present tense verbs?
   ❑ Did you use the present progressive to tell about temporary and continuous activities?

3. *Make your corrections. Rewrite your e-mail message.*

Vocabulary Log

What words or phrases would you like to remember from this chapter? Write five to ten items in your notebook. Examples are on page 10.

Grammar and Punctuation Review

Look over your writing from this chapter. What changes did you need to make in grammar and punctuation? Write them in your notebook. Review them before the next writing assignment.

Chapter 14

Short and Sweet

Many people write e-mail messages instead of letters. It can be very satisfying to get a quick reply to a personal e-mail message. In this chapter you will practice writing e-mail messages and you will learn how to make them more personal.

Starting Point

Smileys

The tone of e-mail communications can be cold and unemotional. One very informal way to add emotion to e-mail messages is to use "emoticons," or "smileys"—typed little facelike designs. Here are some typical emotions. Turn the page 90 degrees to the right to read them.

    : -)   User is happy.

    : - (User is sad or disappointed.

    :*   User is sending kisses.

    ; -)   User is winking or joking.

    8 -)   User is very surprised.

Work with a classmate. Draw lines to match the meanings to these smileys.

1. % -)
2. : - {}
3. : ' - (
4. | - O
5. | - D
6. : - [
7. =: -)

   a. User has a mustache.

   b. User has been staring at the computer screen for 15 hours.

   c. User is a punk rocker.

   d. User is crying.

   e. User is depressed.

   f. User is laughing.

   g. User is yawning.

More E-mail Messages

Although e-mail messages are short, they can communicate a lot of information.

1. *Read the following e-mail messages. Try to figure out, or* **infer,** *how the writers are feeling. Add one appropriate emoticon to an informal message.*

a.

To: abrown@aol.com
From: Campers <user@camprockies.org>
Subject: Help!

Mom and Dad:

The food is terrible, it's raining all the time, and there are really mean kids at this camp. I want to come home! Do I have to stay the whole two weeks? I'm glad they have e-mail here. Reply ASAP.

Alex

P.S. Could you fax me the baseball scores for last night's game?

READING TIP

Be sure to check the *To, From,* and *Subject* lines before you read the text. This will prepare you to understand the situation described in the message.

b.

To: Tom Hanks <thanks@aol.com>
From: Cynthia Lin <cylin@u.washington.edu>
Subject: *Sleepless in Seattle.*

Tom Hanks:

You don't know me, but I got your e-mail address from a book, E-Mail of the Rich and Famous, and I just wanted to tell you how great you were in *Sleepless in Seattle.*

This movie was very popular in Taiwan. In fact, that's why I decided to study in Seattle. I have even been to the houseboat from the movie. It looks a lot different in real life.

Did you like Seattle when you were here making the movie?

Your fan,
Cynthia Lin

c.

To: Helen Ruffin <hruffin@advise.com>
From: Catharine Rimple <catrimp@edota.com>
Subject: Appointment Next Week

Dr. Ruffin:

Do you have any appointment times available next week? I know you are busy, but I'm feeling very depressed and can't seem to pull myself out of it. Can you fit me in your schedule?

Thank you,
Catharine Rimple

d.

To: Mr. President <President@whitehouse.gov>
From: Daniel Lee <dlee@aol.com>
Subject: Tax Increase

Mr. President:

I am writing to express my strong feelings about increasing taxes. Our family can hardly make it with our current after-tax income. Your proposed tax increase will make it impossible for us. Please reconsider your plan and don't increase our taxes.

Sincerely,
Daniel Lee

e.

To: Frank Padilla <fpadilla@tv7.com>
From: Beatrice Costa <beacosta@star.com>
Subject: Thanks!

Honey:

Thanks again for an incredibly romantic evening. The flowers, the meal, the candlelight, the view of the water -- I will never forget it. You are the most thoughtful man I have ever met. I love you!

See you next weekend!
B

f.

To: Dave Bonner <dbonner@orega.com>
From: Party 2 <party2@mtmiska.org>
Subject: View

Dave:

We've had a great climb every step of the way. The view is incredible from Camp One. Sorry you couldn't join us this time. We really miss you, man. Hope your leg is better for our next trip. Tomorrow we start the really tough climbing. I'll send you a message when we get to the summit.

Your buddy,
Jim

P.S. Don't send me any news about the temperature in California. It's really cold up here!

g.

To: Office Bulletin Board <obb@gomish.com>
From: Bob Frank <bfrank@gomish.com>
Subject: New Office Assistant

I'd like to introduce you to Myron Cochron, our new office assistant. Myron will be managing our e-mail messages. From now on, if you have a message for the office bulletin board, please send it to his e-mail address: mcochron. Do not post it directly to the bulletin board.

Please stop by and welcome Myron.
Bob

h.

```
To:  Admissions <admiss@ucla.edu>
From:  Horst Egenolf <hegenolf@bremer.u.edu>
Subject:  Admissions Info

I am writing to request an application and information about
your graduate programs in Sociology. I have a BA degree from
Albert Ludwig Universitat in Freiburg, Germany. I would also
like to know about financial aid or the possibility of a teaching
assistantship.

Sincerely,
Horst Egenolf
```

2. *Which message did you add an emoticon to and why? Discuss with a partner.*

3. *Some information you get from a text is not directly stated. You must discover the meaning using clues in the text. This is called* **inferring meaning.** *Discuss these questions with a classmate. Be prepared to explain to the class how you decided on your answer.*

   a. What modern technology is at Camp Rockies?
      a computer with electronic mail and faxing software

   b. Where is Cynthia from?

   c. What kind of doctor do you think Dr. Ruffin is?

   d. Why does the President give his e-mail address to the public?

   e. Are Frank and Beatrice married?

   f. Where is Jim? Why isn't Dave with him?

   g. What will be one of Myron's job responsibilities?

   h. Why does Horst want information on financial aid or a teaching assistantship?

4. In the e-mail messages on pages 117–120, how is e-mail used? Make a list. One use is suggested for you.

(ANSWER KEY)

to communicate with parents from a summer camp

_____

_____

_____

_____

_____

_____

Reading 2

Reach Out and Touch Someone— Electronically

Not everyone is happy with the electronic revolution.

1. *Read the following selection.*

Reach Out and Touch Someone—Electronically

[1] We hear a lot about communication these days. No one is safe from our reach. If we cannot get someone by phone, we leave a message, which reminds that busy person that he or she needs to respond—now! We want fast answers and fast delivery. The questions we send on e-mail or fax or leave on voice mail just won't wait. We don't just want overnight delivery, we want it by 10:30 a.m. the next day! What is happening to us? Is this speed healthy, or is it crazy?

[2] Why don't we write letters anymore? Are our lives too busy? Too stressful? Remember the letters your mother used to get

from Aunt Annie? The letters that made your mother laugh or shake her head, but that she wouldn't let us read? Remember the days when you looked forward to the mail carrier's arrival? Those were the days when you got chatty letters from Grandma with $5.00 carefully tucked in them. She told you about all of her neighbors and who had died since she last wrote. Why aren't people writing letters by hand anymore?

[3] I am not saying the Internet is to blame for this—although we can still hate it, along with TV and big thick hamburgers—just because it is fashionable to do so. The Internet, however, does push the need to "chat" with someone **right away.**

[4] Last week I took an informal letter-writing survey at my local card and stationery shop:

[5] Me: Do you sell much stationery these days?

[6] Sales associate: What?

[7] Me: You know, the paper that comes in a box and that you write letters and stuff on?

[8] Sales associate (a little brighter): Cards?

[9] Me: No, the blank paper. Well, maybe there's Snoopy or kitties or something in the corner, and you write on it and send it to someone and they send one back, and so on.

[10] Sales associate: Oh.

[11] Me (a little desperately): So . . . so, do you sell much?

[12] Sales associate: I'll get the manager.

[13] But I didn't wait around. I went home and wrote a long letter to an old friend, and I included some photos of the two of us. To be on the safe side, I e-mailed her and told her to wait two days, then look in the mailbox.

2. *Follow the directions below.*

These tasks help you to identify the author's feelings in the essay about communication today.

ANSWER KEY

a. In paragraph 1, underline all the words and expressions that are related to time or speed. List them here. (You may not use all the lines.)

_____	_____
_____	_____
_____	_____
_____	_____
_____	_____

b. In paragraph 1, the author is saying that communication is too _____.

3. *Answer these questions to **identify the support** the author gives for her main idea.*

ANSWER KEY

a. In paragraph 2, the author uses several examples. She wants

to show how much people used to _____.

b. The author includes the dialogue with the sales associate to

show that people _____.

c. The author says, "To be on the safe side, I e-mailed her . . . "

to show how much the author _____ e-mail, too.

> **READING TIP**
>
> As you read an example, ask yourself, "Why did the writer use this example?" This will help you understand the writer's main point.

4. *According to the reading, which of the following statements are true? Write **T** for true and **F** for false.*

a. _____ It's popular to like hamburgers these days.

b. _____ Some people want letters delivered in 24 hours.

c. _____ The author's Aunt Annie wrote funny letters to her.

d. _____ The author probably doesn't get many personal letters in the mail anymore.

e. _____ The Internet allows us to send messages very quickly.

f. _____ The author surveyed salespeople at various card and stationery shops.

g. _____ Stationery is a box that you write on.

Writing

Preparing to Write: Recognizing Tone

Although the writing in e-mail messages is often informal, you will need to use more formal language in certain situations.

1. *To which people would you send an e-mail message with more formal language? Put checks on the lines next to them.*

_____ your doctor

_____ your boss

_____ your friend

_____ your teacher

_____ your officemates (regarding getting together after work)

_____ your employees (regarding a new office policy)

_____ a person you don't know

2. *Two characteristics of more formal e-mail messages are complete sentences and polite expressions. What makes some of the e-mail messages on pages 117–120 more formal? Underline the formal language in these three messages:*

Message C: Catharine Rimple to Dr. Ruffin

Message D: Daniel Lee to the President

Message G: Bob Frank to the employees (via office bulletin board)

3. *Some of these expressions are more formal. Decide which ones are more formal and put checks on the lines next to them.*

(ANSWER KEY)

a. _____ Thank you for your message.

b. _____ I'm writing to let you know . . .

c. _____ Hey! You forgot . . .

d. _____ Thanks!

e. _____ See you soon!
Linda

f. _____ Looking forward to meeting you in person next week,
Mark Ling

g. _____ I'd appreciate your assistance with this.

h. _____ Thanks a lot for your help with this.

Writing an E-mail Message

Choose one of the following tasks.
Write an e-mail message to a famous person.

or

Write an e-mail reply in response to one of the messages in the reading "More E-mail Messages" or to "Reach Out and Touch Someone— Electronically, " by Barbara Combs (Scene@SeattleTimes.com).

_____

_____

_____

_____

> **WRITING TIP**
>
> Although the writing in e-mail messages is often informal, you should write in a formal tone to people you don't know or to people you have a professional relationship with.

Editing and Rewriting

Editing for Sufficient Information

If you are careful to respond specifically to each part of an e-mail message, your e-mail reply should contain enough information to satisfy the person who receives it.

Work with a partner. Follow the directions for each task.

1. Read this request from Margot Elise.

> To: ESL Programs <esl@u.colorado.edu>
> From: Margot Elise <melise@suchet.fr>
>
> Dear ESL Programs:
>
> Please send me information, application, etc.
>
> Thank you very much.
> Margot Elise

Is there enough information in this request? _____

If not, what is missing? _____

2. Reread this message from Catharine Rimple to Dr. Ruffin.

> Dr. Ruffin:
>
> Do you have any appointment times available next week? I know you are busy, but I'm feeling very depressed and can't seem to pull myself out of it. Can you fit me in your schedule?
>
> Thank you,
>
> Catharine Rimple

Dr. Ruffin:

Do you have any appointment times available next week? I know you are busy, but I'm feeling very depressed and can't seem to pull myself out of it. Can you fit me in your schedule?

Thank you,

Catharine Rimple

Is this a sufficient response? _____

If not, what information is missing?

_____

_____

Editing Checklist

Check the Content

1. *Exchange your e-mail message from page 125 with a classmate. After you read your classmate's message, answer these questions.*

   ❏ Is this message appropriate and short?
   ❏ Is there enough information?

   If it's a reply:

   ❏ Have you included the main points of the original message?
   ❏ Is the tone appropriate (formal or informal)?

Check the Details

2. *Reread your e-mail message. If necessary, revise what you wrote. Then continue checking your own writing. Use these questions.*

   ❏ Did you write a word or phrase for the subject line?
   ❏ Did you leave a space between paragraphs?
   ❏ Is the present tense used for habits, facts, and general truths?
   ❏ Is there an **-s** or **-es** ending for third person singular present tense verbs?
   ❏ Did you use the present progressive for temporary or continuous activities?

3. *Make your corrections. Rewrite your e-mail message.*

Vocabulary Log

What words or phrases would you like to remember from this chapter? Write five to ten items in your notebook. Examples are on page 10.

Grammar and Punctuation Review

Look over your writing from this chapter. What changes did you need to make in grammar and punctuation? Write them in your notebook. Review them before the next writing assignment.

Class Activity   Mock E-mail

If you don't have e-mail access at your school, spend some class time sending handwritten "e-mail" messages to and from classmates and your instructor.

1 Give everyone a stack of blank notepaper, all the same size.

2 Include *To, From,* and *Subject* line on each message.

3 No talking! All communication must be in writing.

Chapter 15

E-mail in the Office

It's true that e-mail makes life easier in the office, but it also causes some problems. In this chapter you will read about problems with e-mail and write a new policy for e-mail use in the office.

Starting Point

Problem Solving

1. *Read the following description of an office situation.*

   You are the manager of a large company, Beacon Sales, Inc. E-mail has become very popular among the employees. However, you are worried about the number of hours workers spend reading and sending personal e-mail messages. Last year your company started looking at employees' computer screens through a central computer, and you were shocked to find out the amount of time workers spend on e-mail. In fact, some employees spend half the day on personal e-mail. This lost time costs the company money. The workers need to be more productive during work hours.

2. *Discuss these questions with your classmates.*

   a. What is the basic problem?
   b. What are some possible solutions?
   c. Do you think it is a good idea for managers to secretly read employees' e-mail messages?
   d. How strict should a company be? Should management say: "This is our policy: If you spend time on personal e-mail at work, you will lose your job."? Or should it say: "This is our policy: Please be more careful not to spend time on personal e-mail at work. We appreciate your cooperation."?

Reading

E-mail Snooping in the Workplace

New technology always leads to new legal issues. Is it against the law for managers to snoop on their employees—to read messages between employees without the employees' knowledge? Do managers have the right to read any messages sent within their company?

1. *Read what a court in Pennsylvania decided about e-mail snooping within a company.*

E-mail Snooping in the Workplace

[1] Watch what you write on e-mail at work! A court in Pennsylvania has decided that managers can read any e-mail messages sent on the company computer system. They don't even have to tell employees that they are snooping.

[2] This decision was based on a situation at the Pillsbury Company. Managers saw a printout of an employee's message. They thought the message was inappropriate, and they decided to read all of his e-mail. Then they fired him because he was using e-mail to attack his bosses.

[3] According to the court, Pillsbury's need to prevent unprofessional comments was stronger than the employee's privacy rights. The Pennsylvania decision is similar to two earlier cases in California. This will be good news for some managers. In fact, a recent survey of 500 managers showed that 36 percent of them look at their employees' e-mail.

2. *According to this report, is it legal for managers to read any e-mail messages sent within their company?* _____

3. *For each sentence use* **context clues** *to find a word in the reading with the same meaning as the definition in parentheses. These are all common workplace terms.*

   a. The company had 300 _____. (people who work in a company)

   b. The top _____ in the company discussed the situation and made a decision. (high-level people)

   c. When the supervisor saw someone taking a nap at work, she went to the manager. The manager _____ the employee. (dismissed from his or her job)

   d. The company didn't have a workplace clothing policy, but managers decided that very short skirts looked _____. (not appropriate for the workplace)

4. *According to the court, which was more important in the situation described in the reading?*

ANSWER KEY

_____ **a.** the employee's right to privacy

_____ **b.** the company's need to control inappropriate communication

5. *What is your opinion? Should companies be able to read their employees' e-mail messages? Discuss this issue with your classmates.*

···

Some companies have policies about the use of personal e-mail in the office. These exercises give you practice with vocabulary for office e-mail policies.

1. *Here are some common expressions to use when you are writing a policy announcement. Match the beginning of each sentence in column A with a logical ending from column B. Write the letter of the logical ending on the line.*

Targeting

Expressions for Business Writing

ANSWER KEY

A	**B**
a. As you all know,	_____ please call or e-mail me.
b. As we use personal e-mail more,	___*a*___ e-mail is very popular.
c. We have instituted a new policy	_____ regarding personal e-mail messages.
d. We hope that	_____ the company loses more work time.
e. If you have any questions,	_____ your cooperation in this matter.
f. We would appreciate	_____ this will not continue.

2. *Finish these sentences using items from column A in exercise 1. Be sure that your sentences are complete.*

a. _____ your help in making this new policy work.

b. _____ regarding the use of personal e-mail communications during work hours.

c. _____ e-mail has become a very convenient way to communicate at work.

d. _____ office romances become more possible.

e. _____ come to the discussion on Wednesday at 2 p.m. in the lounge.

f. _____ this will not require that managers screen all e-mail messages.

Writing

Preparing to Write: Planning the New E-mail Policy

Imagine that you are the manager of Beacon Sales, Inc. (see Starting Point, page 129). Your job is to come up with a new policy about the use of personal e-mail in the office and to write a policy announcement.

1. *Answer these questions as you plan the message.*

a. What will the subject line for the policy message be?

_____

b. Why does the company need a new policy?

_____

_____

c. What are your ideas for a new policy regarding personal use of e-mail?

_____

d. What do you hope will happen after this new policy is in place?

_____

_____

On a separate piece of paper, write your policy announcement as an e-mail message.

Writing an Announcement of New Policy

Editing and Rewriting

Editing for Errors with Noncount Nouns

Noncount nouns are rarely plural. It's easy to make mistakes with these nouns.

1. *Review the information in the chart about both count and noncount nouns.*

Rules	Examples
Most nouns in English are **count nouns.** They name things that can be counted.	a **computer** three **messages** many **phone lines**
Count nouns can be singular, or they can have a plural **-s** or **-es** ending. They can combine with plural expressions such as **many, several, ten.**	**many** computers **several** messages **ten** phone lines
Some nouns in English are **noncount nouns.** They name things that are not counted.	new **software** a lot of **information** our **cooperation** no **mail**
Noncount nouns are almost always singular; they are rarely plural. Noncount nouns can combine with quantity expressions such as **much, a lot of, a little.**	We have **a lot of** new software. There isn't **much** information. I need **a little** help.

> See page 200 in Reference for more information about **noncount nouns**.

2. *Put a (✓) next to the three correct noun phrases.*

   a. _____ a policy

   b. _____ an information

   c. _____ a computer

   d. _____ a mail

   e. _____ two letters in my mailbox

   f. _____ no mails today

   g. _____ some more softwares

3. *Correct the noun errors in these sentences.*

   a. There are ten computer in this lab.

   b. I would appreciate your cooperations in this matter.

   c. "Snail" mails are slower than e-mail.

   d. This wastes a lot of company times.

   e. There are much advantages to e-mail.

   f. There is more softwares in the storeroom.

   g. I got some informations today.

   h. We have instituted a new policy regarding company use of e-mails.

   i. There are so many message in my mailbox that I'll never get through them today.

Editing Checklist

Check the Content

1. *Exchange your e-mail policy announcement from page 133 with a classmate. After you read your classmate's announcement, answer these questions.*

   ❏ Is there a subject line? Is it a phrase, not a sentence?
   ❏ Is the reason for the new policy clear?
   ❏ Is there an explanation of how the new policy works?
   ❏ Does the announcement end with a wish for cooperation?

Check the Details

2. *Reread your e-mail policy announcement. If necessary, revise what you wrote, then continue checking your own writing. Use these questions.*

   ❏ Is the present tense used to write about habits, facts, and general truths?
   ❏ Is there an **-s** or **-es** ending for third person singular present tense verbs?
   ❏ Did you use the present progressive to write about temporary or continuous activities?
   ❏ Are the noncount nouns singular? Did you use quantity expressions with the noncount nouns?

3. *Make your corrections. Rewrite your e-mail message.*

Vocabulary Log

What words or phrases would you like to remember from this chapter? Write five to ten items in your notebook. Examples are on page 10.

Grammar and Punctuation Review

Look over your writing from this chapter. What changes did you need to make in grammar and punctuation? Write them in your notebook. Review them before the next writing assignment.

A Fish Out of Water

When we go to live in another place, we experience many differences. This change is both exciting and difficult. We may feel out of place—like a "fish out of water." Some people call this experience of change *culture shock*.

In the next three chapters, you will do these activities:

- Read a description of culture shock
- Read letters to and from people living abroad
- Write a description of an experience in a new culture
- Write a letter of advice

Chapter 16

Cultural Adjustment

What kinds of things are different in a new place? Some cultural changes are difficult and may be hard for you to adjust to. In this chapter you will read about this difficult adjustment in a description and in a personal letter.

Starting Point

What's Different?

When you live in or visit another country, you see lots of differences.

1. *Think about your experience in another country. Complete this chart.*

	Your Country	*New Country*
Food		
Transportation		
Money		
Stores/Shopping		
People's customs		

2. *Work with a partner. Discuss your charts. How did you feel about the differences between the countries? Have your feelings changed over time? How did they change?*

Reading

Culture Shock

Many people experience different stages of cultural adjustment in a new country.

1. *Read the following selection.*

Culture Shock

[1] When you live in a different place, especially in another culture, you will probably experience culture shock. All of the familiar parts of your old life—language, customs, food, weather—are no longer the same. You feel like a fish out of water.

[2] Adjusting to a new culture is not the same for everyone. However, most people experience cultural adjustment in four stages: (1) the honeymoon stage, (2) the hostility stage, (3) the humor stage, and (4) the home stage.

[3] When you first get to the new culture, you are in the honeymoon stage. You are happy, and you are enjoying all of your new life. You are excited to learn about your new world and to have all kinds of experiences. Everything is interesting. When you write home, you tell people about all of the wonderful things in your new life.

[4] In the second stage, the hostility stage, you experience culture shock. You seem to get angry about little things. You get upset and frustrated often. There are many things you don't like. The food is not good, the people aren't friendly, and the weather is terrible! You feel very alone, you don't sleep well, and you miss many things from your old home. At this point, you remember only the good things about home.

[5] After a while, you get over the difficult culture shock stage. You are even able to laugh at yourself. You remember the mistakes you made with the language and customs, but now these mistakes are funny to you. You understand why people in the new culture do things the way they do. This is stage 3: the humor stage.

[6] Finally, you feel at home with the new culture. It doesn't feel like your real home, but you are comfortable living there. This is the home stage: You don't like everything, but you are used to the language and the culture.

2. *Choose the correct answer.*

A fish out of water means _____.

   a. near death
   b. in the wrong place
   c. on a wild adventure
   d. completely out of place; awkward

3. Work with a partner. Look at the following pictures of Takeshi's experience as he gets used to life in Saudi Arabia. Discuss these pictures. According to the stages of cultural adjustment in the reading, what stage (1, 2, 3, or 4) do you think Takeshi is experiencing in each picture? **Apply the information** you learned in the reading to help you choose the answers. Write the numbers on the lines.

a. _____

b. _____

c. _____

d. _____

4. *The sentences below are statements made by people who are adjusting to a new culture. Write the stage of cultural adjustment in the blank next to each comment.*

a. "I'm so sick of the cold and rain!" _____*hostility stage*_____

b. "I'm dreaming in English! I speak it without thinking about it!"

_____

c. "I was trying to get to the Modern Art Museum. A woman on the bus gave me directions and walked with me to the museum! People are so friendly here!"

_____

d. "Everything I eat tastes the same. They put the same sauce on everything!" _____

e. "Remember the time I was trying to say *snack*, but I kept saying *snake*? My host family didn't understand me, and I felt so stupid. I laugh every time I remember it now!"

_____

5. *Read this description of Lesley's situation.*

Lesley is studying Portuguese in Brazil. In her first letters home, she seemed to be very happy about life in Brazil. Her mother hasn't heard from her for more than a month. Now, her mother is worried that Lesley is experiencing culture shock.

Read the letter from Lesley's mother. **Apply the information** *you learned in the reading. Underline all of the symptoms of culture shock.*

Dear Lesley,   March 6, 1998

How are you? Everything is fine here at home. We've noticed a change in your letters, and we're wondering if everything is okay with you. Your first letters were wonderful. You described your new life so vividly, and we felt like we were there with you. Now you sound a little sad. Are you feeling homesick? Are you bored?

Do you remember when Dad had to work in Germany for six months? He says that he had a lot of trouble sleeping. That made everything worse. He felt better after he started to get more exercise. Exercising helped him sleep better. Are you sleeping well?

You also sounded kind of negative about things (your host mother's cooking can't be that bad!) I bet that you'll feel better about things when you get used to the different way that people do things there. You'll probably even have a hard time adjusting to life back here after your time away!

Try to remember that it's all a learning experience – it may seem difficult now, but you'll look back at it and remember the interesting things. Someday, you'll probably tell a lot of funny stories about your experiences there, although I'm sure they don't seem very funny now.

Please call us next week. We'll be home every night. We'll be looking forward to hearing your voice!

Love,
Mom

6. *Answer these questions about Lesley.*

    a. Why do you think Lesley hasn't written? What are some possibilities?

    b. How is she probably feeling?

    c. What stage of cultural adjustment do you think Lesley is in?

Targeting

Words to Describe Emotions

We use many words to say how we feel. Some of these words indicate good feelings, and some indicate upsetting or unhappy feelings.

With a classmate, put a plus sign (+) next to the positive (good) adjectives and a minus sign (–) next to the negative (bad) adjectives. Use +/– if the adjective may be either positive or negative.

___ happy	___ interested	___ bored
___ excited	___ homesick	___ uncomfortable
___ interesting	___ wonderful	___ comfortable
___ upset	___ angry	___ isolated
___ optimistic	___ frustrated	___ awkward
___ terrible	___ alone	___ self-conscious
___ friendly	___ challenged	

Quickwriting: Experiencing Culture Shock

How did you feel about your first few weeks in a different culture? In your notebook, write for five or ten minutes about this question.

Vocabulary Log

What words or phrases would you like to remember from this chapter? Write five to ten items in your notebook. Examples are on page 10.

Chapter 17

Fireflies or City Lights? Getting Over Culture Shock

Starting Point

How can you overcome culture shock? Do people only experience it in another country? In this chapter you will read about adjusting to urban and rural life. You will also write a description of a personal experience adjusting to a different culture.

Giving Advice

There is no one way to overcome culture shock because each person is different, but the suggestions in this section might help.

1. *Work with a partner. First, look at the illustration. After you read all the ideas, circle the five best ones.*

Keep busy.
Speak your native language sometimes.
Spend some time alone.
Join a club or church.
Do sports.
Try to meet new people, even people who are also new to the culture.
Accept the idea that you have culture shock.
Treat yourself to something special.
Don't try so hard. Be patient with yourself.
Keep working on learning the language.
Spend some time with people from your own culture.
Don't lose your sense of humor. Try to see what is funny in your new life.
Keep your mind open. Be ready to learn new things.
Realize that different doesn't mean better or worse.
Show interest in other's conversations. Ask questions. Be a good listener.
Talk to someone about your feelings.

2. *What advice in exercise 1 would be hard for you to follow? Why? Talk about your answers with a classmate.*

ANSWER KEY

3. *Here are some qualities that are important in intercultural adjustment. Match the qualities with their definitions. Write the correct letters on the lines.*

a. a clear, secure feeling of who you are

b. the ability to realize that you will sometimes make mistakes or be less successful than you were at home

c. the ability and willingness to share your feelings and thoughts with others

d. the ability to show warmth to and respect for others

e. the desire to know about other people, places, and ideas

f. the ability to laugh at yourself

g. the ability to expect good things to happen to you rather than bad things

h. the ability to keep your opinions flexible, to be open to other ideas

i. the ability to understand beliefs that are different from your own

_h_ open-mindedness

___ a sense of humor

___ an acceptance of failure

___ communicativeness

___ curiosity

___ positive expectations

___ tolerance

___ positive feelings for others

___ a strong sense of self

4. *Which of the qualities in exercise 3 do you have? Share your response with a classmate.*

Reading

Student Letter

A move to a new place is often difficult to adjust to.

1. *Read the following letter from Gye-Sun to her former ESL classmate Ling-Ling.*

October 5, 1997

Dear Ling-Ling:

How are things in the ESL program? I really miss you, but I am finally settled in at my college in Evansburg. Life here is very different from life in San Francisco. The first couple of weeks I was very depressed. I was just not used to rural life. In fact, I never even lived in the country when I lived in Korea. I'm a city girl! I missed the people on the streets and all the activity. I even missed the traffic! It seemed like there was nothing to do. I was very bored and homesick for city life. I thought I had made a big mistake by coming to this college.

But now that I'm in my classes, I enjoy this quiet, small town and the beautiful campus. Everyone is very friendly. If I walk uptown to buy something, I always see someone I know. It's very safe here, too. I don't even lock my car anymore! Can you imagine that? If I get too used to this, it will be a big shock when I go back to Seoul.

I'd like to show you around this place and introduce you to my new friends. Why don't you come out over the next break? Maybe we could fit in a trip to Chicago, too!

Love,
Gye-Sun

2. One way to organize ideas is to write them around a key word and draw lines to show how they are related. This is called **mapping.** Look at the example below.

Example:

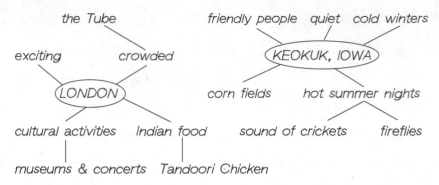

Now map the ideas from the letter in the reading. Write words from the letter around the names below and draw lines to show how these words are related.

3. Underline the correct ending to these statements about Gye-Sun's letter.

    a. According to the reading, Gye-Sun lives in
      1. a big city.
      2. a rural area.
      3. San Francisco.
      4. Seoul.

    b. All of the following statements are true about Gye-Sun *except* that she
      1. is used to living in a big city.
      2. is used to living in a more dangerous area.
      3. is not used to the traffic.
      4. likes crowds of people.

    c. Gye-Sun is worried that she won't be able to adjust to life in
      1. San Francisco anymore.
      2. Seoul again.
      3. this small town.
      4. Chicago someday.

Writing

Sometimes it is difficult to write a description of your own experience. This exercise helps you to organize your ideas before you write.

Preparing to Write: Mapping Ideas

1. *Have you ever experienced the shock of moving from one area to another? Here you will **map your ideas** about that experience. Read all the directions and study the example before you map your ideas.*

   a. *In the blank space below, write the names of the two places you lived. Draw a circle around the words. Leave a lot of space around them on the page. Look at the example from exercise 2 on page 146.*

    b. *Around each name, write all of the words you think of when you remember that place.*

    c. *Some of these words may make you think of other ideas. Use lines to connect ideas to each other. Look again at the example.*

2. *Complete these sentences with ideas from your own experience adjusting to a different place.*

When I first came here/went there, _____

When I spoke to people, _____

Everything was _____

I liked/didn't like _____

The food is/was _____

Sometimes I miss/missed _____

I thought people were _____

Now/After a while, I feel/felt _____

People seem _____

To get over culture shock, I need/needed to _____

I hope in the future _____

_____
(other ideas)

Writing a Description of an Experience

Write a description about your experience adjusting to a different culture. Give lots of details.

....

English sentences express a complete idea.

Editing for Sentence Completeness

1. *Study these rules.*

Rules	Examples
Complete sentences have a subject and verb.	**You shouldn't stay** at home <small>subject verb</small> all weekend. **He is feeling** very depressed. <small>subject verb</small>
The subject in an **imperative sentence**—a request or a command—is *you.*	**Don't stay** at home. <small>verb</small> **Get out** and **talk** to people. <small>verbs</small>

2. *Put a check (✓) in front of the complete sentence(s).*

a. _____   Spend some time by yourself.

b. _____   He came back to my country a month ago.

c. _____   The people from a different culture.

3. *Make these sentences complete—expressing a complete idea with both a subject and a verb.*

a. At home lots of friends and good food.

   At home we have lots of friends and good food.

b. In Mexico City is hotter than in Chicago.

   _____

c. My family and friends there.

   _____

d. Is good to be home.

   _____

e. My mother a very good cook and a very warm person.

_____

f. Likes his new apartment.

_____

g. Now I planning to visit New Zealand.

_____

h. In the country never locked my door.

_____

4. _In exercise 3, underline the words you added to the sentences. Label subjects and verbs, as appropriate. Then work with a partner. Exchange your exercises and check each other's sentences._

Editing Checklist

Check the Content

1. _Exchange your description from page 148 with a classmate. After you read your classmate's description, answer these questions._

❏ Is the description clear and interesting?
❏ Are there enough details about the writer's experience?

Check the Details

2. _Now, reread your description. If necessary, revise your paper. Add more details and descriptive adjectives. Then continue checking your own writing. Use these questions._

❏ Did you use the past tense to write about past experiences?
❏ Did you use the present tense to write about facts, general truths, and habits?
❏ Did you use the present progressive tense to write about temporary or continuous activities?
❏ Are your sentences complete?
❏ Does each sentence have a subject and verb?
❏ Does each sentence begin with a capital letter and end with a period, a question mark, or an exclamation point?

3. _Make your corrections. Rewrite your description._

Vocabulary Log

What words or phrases would you like to remember from this chapter? Write five to ten items in your notebook. Examples are on page 10.

Grammar and Punctuation Review

Look over your writing from this chapter. What changes did you need to make in grammar and punctuation? Write them in your notebook. Review them before the next writing assignment.

Class Activity   Culture Shock Advice

1 New arrivals to your area may need help when they experience culture shock. What would be the best way to give them information and advice? A poster? A brochure? A fact sheet? A list of frequently asked questions and possible answers? Decide which way you would choose to help them.

2 In a group or with a partner, decide how to organize your information. Would illustrations help?

3 Complete your work on this project. If possible, distribute or display it so that new arrivals will benefit from your advice!

Chapter 18

Reverse Culture Shock

It isn't always easy going back to your country after you have lived in another culture. In this chapter you will read about adjusting back to your culture and you will write a letter of advice.

Starting Point

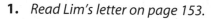

Quickwriting

What do you think happens when a person returns to a country after living abroad for two years? In your notebook, write for five or ten minutes about this question.

Reading

A Student's Letter from Home

Lim, an ESL student, returned to his home in Taipei after he lived in Seattle for two years. He is experiencing reverse culture shock—difficulty readjusting to his own country. Lim wrote a letter to his friend, Koichi, in Seattle.

1. *Read Lim's letter on page 153.*

2. *What can you **infer** about Lim's feelings upon returning home? Which of the following statements are true according to Lim's letter? Write a **T** in the blank for true and an **F** for false.*

   a. __F__ Lim wrote Koichi from Taiwan before he wrote this letter.

   b. ____ Lim was prepared to experience re-entry culture shock.

   c. ____ Koichi was looking for an American girlfriend when Lim was in the United States.

   d. ____ Lim was homesick when he lived in Seattle.

   e. ____ Lim's friends in Taiwan want to hear about Seattle.

   f. ____ Lim's friends in Taiwan expect to be with the Lim they used to know.

June 15, 1997

Dear Koichi:

Sorry that I have taken so long to write back. I had a good trip back and my family is fine. The problem is that it's very hard being in Taipei again. I was so depressed that I couldn't write to any of my ESL friends. I missed my family and friends so much when I lived in the States, and I couldn't wait to get home. Now that I'm home, I feel like a fish out of water! I didn't expect that. I wish you were here, because you would understand. All my Chinese friends are sick of hearing me talk about the good times in Seattle.

I am homesick for all of you. How is everyone? Do you still go to the same club on Friday nights? Are you still looking for an American girlfriend to help you with your English?!!

I just don't know what to do. I am not the same person, and everyone expects me to be the same Lim who left two years ago. I'm sorry I can't write more. I am doing nothing, and it is very boring here.

Please write soon, and have an espresso for me!

Your friend,
Lim

3. *Circle the number of the sentence in each pair that shows the typical feelings of reverse culture shock.*

a. 1. Nobody wants to listen to my stories about life abroad.
2. Everybody wants to listen to my stories about life abroad.

b. 1. Everyone understands the experiences I had.
2. No one understands the experiences I had.

c. 1. I am different, but people treat me like the old me.
2. I am different, and people treat me differently.

d. 1. I feel like a native.
2. I feel like a foreigner in my own country.

e. 1. Everything is uninteresting.
2. Everything is new and exciting.

f. 1. Everything was wonderful where I lived before.
2. Everything was horrible where I lived before.

Writing

Preparing to Write: Advice Expressions

This section gives you practice writing advice expressions. You can use some of these expressions in the next writing assignment, a letter of advice to Lim.

1. *Read this information about advice expressions.*

Rules	Examples
These expressions are often used to give opinions or advice.	**should** **ought to** **If I were you, I'd** **It's a good idea to** **It's a bad idea to**
Be careful about the verb form that follows each one.	You should **talk** to people. You ought to **talk** to people. If I were you, I'd **talk** to people. It's a good idea to **talk** to people.

2. *Combine the advice expressions in the left column with the advice in the right column to make complete sentences. Write the sentences on the lines. More than one combination is possible for some expressions.*

ANSWER KEY

You should	look for other people who have lived abroad.
You ought to	to volunteer to speak at schools about your
It's a good idea	experience.
If I were you, I'd	to stay at home and feel depressed.
It's a bad idea	keep your sense of humor.
	remember you have lived through bad times
	before.

You should keep your sense of humor.

_____

_____

_____

_____

_____

_____

_____

_____

Writing a Letter of Advice

Imagine you were one of Lim's friends in the ESL program. Write a letter of advice to Lim, who is unhappy back in Taiwan. Tell him what he should do to get over reverse culture shock. If you need help, look at the Quickwriting on page 152 and Preparing to Write on page 154.

Editing and Rewriting

Editing for Errors with Count Nouns

Count nouns are nouns that can be singular or plural: **a** friend, **two** friend**s**, **this** book, my English book**s**. A common mistake is to forget the plural **-s** or **-es** for count nouns. When you are editing, look at every noun and decide if it should be plural.

1. *Study this information.*

Rules	Examples
A count noun can never be "bare" or stand alone.	*Incorrect* There are cat here. I have cat. It's cat. Where is cat? We gave cat a name.
A count noun must be "covered" by a plural ending or a determiner.	*Correct* *Add a plural ending:* There are cat**s** here.
A determiner gives **basic** information about a noun. Typical determiners are articles, possessives, demonstratives, and quantifiers.	*Add a determiner:* I have **a** cat. *(article)* It's **my** cat. *(possessive)* Where is **that** cat? *(demonstrative)* We gave **each** cat a name. *(quantifier)*
Adjectives give **extra** information about nouns, but they are not determiners.	*Incorrect:* They are beautiful cat. *Correct:* They are beautiful cat**s**.

Rules	Examples	
	Incorrect	*Correct*
If you have a "bare" count noun in your writing, something is wrong. Ask yourself these questions: 1. What can I add to "cover" this noun? 2. Is the noun really plural? (If it is, add a plural ending.) 3. If the noun is really singular, can I add a determiner? Which determiner?	We are friend. → I have friend. → He's friend. →	We are friend**s**. I have **a** friend. He's **my** friend.

2. *Check every noun in these sentences. Underline the "bare," singular count nouns. Circle any plural signals. Decide if the noun needs a plural -s or -es. Some sentences may be correct.*

   a. There are several stages of cultural adjustment.
   b. When I speak to native speaker, it is difficult to understand them.
   c. I have a great interest in American culture.
   d. He made several change in his pronunciation, and people understood him better.
   e. She had many unpleasant experience on her trip.
   f. I called my friend and talked to them about my new life in Chicago.
   g. San Diego and San Francisco are both very wonderful city.
   h. I try to find a number of way to practice my English.
   i. I remember so many time I dreamed of coming to this country.
   j. Custom are hard to adjust to.

Editing Checklist

Check the Content

1. *Exchange your letter of advice with a classmate. After you read your classmate's letter, answer the question.*

   ❑ Does the advice fit Lim's situation?

Check the Details

2. *Now, reread your letter of advice. Reread Lim's letter and change your advice, if necessary. Then continue checking your own writing. Use these questions.*

   Underline the singular count nouns.
   ❑ Are they really singular or do they need a plural -s or -es?
   ❑ Do they need determiners (articles, possessives, demonstratives, or quantifiers)?

   Underline the verbs.
   ❑ Did you use imperatives or *should* to give advice?
   ❑ Did you use the base form of verbs after advice expressions?
   ❑ Did you use the past tense to write about past experiences?
   ❑ Did you use the present tense to write about facts, general truths, and habits?
   ❑ Did you use the present progressive tense to write about temporary or continuous activities?

3. *Make your corrections. Rewrite your letter of advice.*

Vocabulary Log

What words or phrases would you like to remember from this chapter? Write five to ten items in your notebook. Examples are on page 10.

Grammar and Punctuation Review

Look over your writing from this chapter. What changes did you need to make in grammar and punctuation? Write them in your notebook. Review them before the next writing assignment.

6 Issues in Family Life

Is it better to marry young or to wait until you are well-established in a job? Is day care good for children? What is the best way to teach or to discipline children? Is family life really easier now than it was fifty years ago? This section deals with some major issues and changes in family life today.

In this unit you will do these activities:

- Read and write about the best age for getting married and having children

- Consider a difficult situation for a young child and write your opinion in a formal letter

- Read a poem about memories of being punished as a child

- Read about theories of discipline

- Read about why one spouse complains and another doesn't

- Write about whether family life is easier or harder now than it was in the past

Chapter 19

The Best Age?

In countries all over the world, people are getting married and having children later in life. In this chapter you will read about one person's experience with parenthood and write your opinion.

Starting Point

Identifying Relationships

Look at the photograph. How do you think these people are related? Discuss with a partner.

Reading

One Woman's Perspective

This reading selection gives one person's opinion and describes a family situation that is becoming common in the United States—people becoming parents at older ages.

1. *Read the following selection.*

One Woman's Perspective

[1] I had my first child at age forty-one. My husband was forty-nine. What a surprise! We both had mixed feelings when we found out that I was pregnant. Would the baby be healthy? Would the baby change our lives in a positive or a negative way?

[2] We were very lucky. Our daughter is healthy, and she is a wonderful addition to our lives. I am not sure what kind of mother I would have been at twenty or thirty, but I find that, at forty-plus, I have a lot of patience for my daughter and her friends. After working for so many years, money is not a problem for us, so I work only part-time. I feel like I enjoy (almost!) every minute with my daughter.

[3] Is this the perfect age to have children? There is a downside. I can't read the labels on the baby food jars without glasses, and I'm the oldest mother in the neighborhood, but I'm not complaining!

READING TIP

Sometimes the author's main point is given in the first or last sentence of a para-graph. Other times, **main ideas** are not stated directly. The reader has to figure them out, or **infer** them.

2. *Finding the writer's **main idea** is an important reading skill. Complete the sentence. Write the letter of the main idea on the line.*

   In general, the writer thinks that _____.

   a. people should think seriously before having a child when they are past forty.
   b. it is fine to have children when you are older.
   c. age forty-plus is the perfect time to have children.

3. *Write a **T** in the blank if the sentence is true, **F** if it is false.*

   a. _____ The woman and her husband were both middle-aged when they had their child.

   b. _____ The woman also had a child when she was twenty or thirty.

   c. _____ She and her husband are not worried about money.

   d. _____ She worked part-time before she had a child.

   e. _____ Occasionally, she does not enjoy being with her daughter.

   f. _____ She has trouble reading without glasses because of her age.

4. *Find words in the reading that mean the same as the words or expressions below. Write them on the lines.*

In Paragraph 1

a. both positive and negative   *mixed*

b. the two of us

c. unexpected event

d. going to have a child

e. bad

In Paragraph 2

f. type

g. feeling of calm while waiting

h. difficult thing

i. most all of the

In Paragraph 3

j. best

k. negative aspect

l. printed information

m. saying something negative

Writing

Discussing opinions helps you organize your thoughts before you
write about the topic—the best age for getting married and having
children.

**Preparing to Write:
Discussing Opinions**

Complete these sentences. Then discuss your opinions with a classmate.

a. I think the best age for women to get married is _____

because _____.

b. I think the best age for men to get married is _____

because _____.

c. I think the best age for women to have children is _____

because _____.

d. I think the best age for men to have children is_____

because _____.

Writing an Opinion

Choose one of the ideas from your discussion. Write about your opinion.

Editing and Rewriting

Transition Words Introducing Reasons and Examples

Reasons and examples support your opinions and help make your ideas clear. They can be introduced with transition words, or words that join two sentence elements.

1. *Study these rules and examples. The words in boldface are transition words.*

Rules	*Examples*
Because introduces a reason. It connects two clauses. When the **because** clause comes first, put a comma after it.	They were excited **because** they wanted to have children. **Because** they wanted children, they were very excited.
So introduces a result. Do not begin a sentence with **so.**	They wanted to have children, **so** they were very excited.
Therefore is a more formal word to introduce a result. Separate **therefore** from the rest of the sentence with a comma.	They wanted to have children. **Therefore,** they were very excited.
For example and **such as** introduce examples. Separate **for example** from the rest of the sentence with a comma. Use **such as** before nouns, not clauses.	Older parents provide more security for their children. **For example,** they have worked longer, and they probably have more money saved. Older parents usually don't have to worry about basic things **such as** finances or jobs.

For more information about **transitions,** see pages 201–202 in Reference.

2. *Put a check (✓) in front of the sentence(s) that are correct.*

a. _____ They were worried. Because she was over forty.

b. _____ The doctor gave her additional tests because she was over forty.

c. _____ So they were very excited.

d. _____ The test results were fine, so they were happy.

e. _____ Women over thirty-five have a greater chance of having babies with birth defects. Therefore, their doctors usually give them additional tests.

f. _____ Pregnant women should give up things that are bad for the baby, such as alcohol and cigarettes.

g. _____ Pregnant women need healthful food. For example, they need to drink a lot of milk.

3. Complete the sentences with **because, so, for example, therefore,** or **such as.**

   a. They were worried <u>because</u> they were middle-aged.

   b. They had lived without children for a long time, _____ they had mixed feelings.

   c. The doctor gave her tests to check for possible problems _____ birth defects or inherited conditions.

   d. Money was not a problem, _____ she worked only part-time.

   e. She did find some challenges. _____, she was older than many of the other first-time mothers.

   f. _____ she has a lot of patience, she enjoys being with her daughter.

   g. The print on the labels is very small, _____ she has trouble reading them.

   h. Older parents _____ this woman are becoming more common.

   i. As people get older, they have a hard time reading small print. _____, they often need to wear glasses to read.

4. Correct the errors in the following sentences. Some errors are in word order and word choice, and some are in punctuation. You may need to add words.

                                For example, they went to

   a. Before they had the baby, they traveled a lot. ~~such as~~ Canada
       and the United States last year.   ^

   b. They were tired because they stayed home.

c. They decided to save money for their daughter's education. Therefore they stopped going out to eat every day.

d. They used to eat out a lot because they saved a lot of money when they stopped going out to eat.

e. They wanted to send their children to college. So they needed to save money.

f. Because they wanted to send them to private school they had to save a lot of money.

Editing Checklist

Check the Content

1. *Exchange your opinion writing with a classmate. After you read what your classmate wrote, answer these questions.*

   ❏ Are the opinions clear?
   ❏ Are there enough details?

Check the Details

2. *Reread your writing. If necessary, revise what you wrote. Try to add more reasons or examples. Then continue checking your own writing. Use these questions.*

   ❏ Did you use transition words and expressions to give examples or explain reasons? Check the punctuation with these transitions.
   ❏ Check each verb. Is the tense correct? Is the form correct?

3. *Make your corrections. Rewrite your opinion.*

Vocabulary Log

What words or phrases would you like to remember from this chapter? Write five to ten items in your notebook. Examples are on page 10.

Grammar and Punctuation Review

Look over your writing from this chapter. What changes did you need to make in grammar and punctuation? Write them in your notebook. Review them before the next writing assignment.

Chapter 20

Caring for the Children

Starting Point

Many different people take care of children, from parents to day care workers. What happens when parents get divorced? Who should have custody of the children? In this chapter you will read about a child custody situation and write your opinion in a formal letter.

Who Are the Caregivers?

Children's caregivers can be their parents, other family members, or people hired to take care of them.

1. *Who is taking care of these children? Match the photographs with the caregivers listed on the right. Write the words under the pictures.*

mother or father

day care workers

grandparents

nursery school teacher

nanny or babysitter

2. *Fill in the lines to answer these questions about your own childhood.*

    a. Who took care of you when you were a young child?

       When I was a very young child, _____ took care of me.

    b. Did that situation change when you got a little older? If so, how?

       At age _____ , _____.

       _____.

    c. What did you do after school each day? Was your mother at home after school?

       After school each day, _____.

3. *Discuss your answers to exercises 1 and 2 with a partner or a small group.*

Sometimes family life is very complicated. This reading describes a difficult situation for two divorced parents and their daughter.

1. *Read the following selection.*

What's Best for Maranda?

[1] Steven Smith and Jennifer Ireland, at ages seventeen and sixteen, got married and had a daughter, Maranda. A short time later, they got divorced. Steven went back to live with his parents. Jennifer and Maranda lived with Jennifer's mother.

[2] When her little girl was three years old, Jennifer got a scholarship from the University of Michigan in Ann Arbor. This city was about three hours away from Jennifer's mother's house. Jennifer did not want to be away from Maranda, so she and Maranda both moved to Ann Arbor. Every day, when Jennifer was in class, Maranda went to a day care center. On weekends and vacations, they went home to stay with Jennifer's mother.

[3] Steven Smith was attending a community college and living with his parents. He got help from a lawyer. They went to court and asked a judge to give Steven custody of Maranda. He wanted her to live at his parents' home. His mother, a full-time homemaker, wanted to take care of Maranda while Steven was in classes at college.

The next exercise asks you to give your opinion about Maranda's situation. To do this, you will have to **evaluate the information** in the reading.

2. *To evaluate what is best for Maranda, complete this chart with facts from the reading. Then evaluate the situations. In your opinion, what are the advantages (+) and disadvantages (−) of each? List them in the chart.*

With Jennifer	*With Steven's Mother*
_____ take(s) care of Maranda. If Jennifer goes home on weekends, _____ will also help out.	_____ care of Maranda.

+	−	+	−
_____	_____	_____	_____
_____	_____	_____	_____
_____	_____	_____	_____
_____	_____	_____	_____
_____	_____	_____	_____
_____	_____	_____	_____
_____	_____	_____	_____

ANSWER KEY

3. *Complete these sentences with words from the reading.*

   a. Steven Smith and Jennifer Ireland _____

      _____ when they were very young.

b. They decided in just a short time to _____

_____ .

c. At first Jennifer and Maranda _____ _____

Jennifer's mother.

d. However, Jennifer _____ _____

_____ from the University of Michigan.

e. When Jennifer moved to Ann Arbor, she put Maranda in a

_____ _____ _____.

f. Steven _____ _____ _____ a

lawyer.

g. He wanted to _____ _____ of Maranda.

h. Steven's mother was a full-time _____ , so Steven

thought she could _____ _____

_____ Maranda better than the people at a day

care center could.

Reflect on Reading

You **evaluated information** in exercise 2. Evaluating information is a critical thinking skill. To evaluate what you read, ask yourself questions: What do I think about this? Do I agree with the writer? In which of these situations would evaluating information be important? Discuss with a partner or a small group.

Reading the newspaper
Reading a textbook for a course
Reading a science fiction novel

Targeting

Ways to Express Opinions

Here are some typical ways to express opinions about this case.

1. *Complete the sentences with your ideas. Be careful with the verb forms following **should** and in **if** clauses.*

    a. I agree with _____.
        (Steven or Jennifer)

    I disagree with _____.
        (Jennifer or Steven)

    b. Maranda should _____ with _____
        mother.   *(your opinion)*

    c. If Maranda _____ with her mother,

    _____.
        (your idea)

    d. If Maranda _____ to her father,

    _____.
        (your idea)

    e. Living with _____ is the best situation for
        (your idea for the best person)
        Maranda.

    f. If Jennifer _____ custody of Maranda, _____.
                                                      (your idea)

    g. If Steven _____ custody of Maranda, _____.
                                                      (your idea)

    h. The judge should _____ custody of Maranda to her

    _____ . The judge _____ give custody of
        (your opinion)   *(shouldn't/should)*
        Maranda to her _____.

Writing

Preparing to Write: Making a Decision

The judge in this case gave a ruling about Maranda's care.

1. *Read about the decision in this case.*

In the custody battle between Steven Smith and Jennifer Ireland, Judge Raymond Cashen ruled last week that Maranda Ireland Smith should live with her father's family. In making his decision, Judge Cashen said that Maranda's paternal grandmother would give her the best care. If Maranda continued to live with her mother, she would have to spend time in day care, where strangers would be taking care of her.

2. *What is your opinion of the judge's decision? Discuss your opinion with your classmates.*

Write a letter to Judge Raymond T. Cashen, Macomb County Courthouse, 40 N. Main, Mt. Clemens, MI 48143. Tell him whether you agree or disagree with his decision. Use formal business letter style.

a. *Here are two possible sentences you could use to start your letter. Don't forget to give your reasons.*

1. I am writing to congratulate you on your decision in the Maranda Ireland Smith case.

2. I am outraged by your decision to separate Maranda Ireland Smith from her mother.

b. *Here are two possible sentences for concluding (final) statements.*

1. I am sorry that more judges don't have the courage to take a stand as you did in this decision.

2. I certainly hope that Jennifer Ireland's lawyer will appeal this shameful decision to a higher court.

Writing a Letter to Express an Opinion

> **WRITING TIP**
>
> In most business letters, writers do not indent the beginning of a paragraph. Instead, they leave an extra space between paragraphs.

Editing and Rewriting

Editing for Verb Tense and Punctuation in *If* and Time Clauses

We often use *when, if, before, after,* or *until* to talk about conditions or explain when something happens. In these clauses, be careful with punctuation and with the verb form.

1. *Study these rules.*

Rules	Examples
If the **time** or *if* **clause** is at the beginning of the sentence, you need a comma after the clause.	**When people get divorced,** they sometimes argue about their children. **When my parents got divorced,** my father fought for custody of us. **If single parents need to work,** it's sometimes difficult for them to take care of the children.
If the **time** or *if* **clause** is at the end of the sentence, you do not need a comma.	I visited my father every other weekend **after my parents got divorced.** Sometimes it's difficult for a single parent to take care of the children **if he or she needs to work.**
Be careful with the verb when the meaning in the *if* or time clause is the future. We usually use the **present tense** to describe the future in the time or *if* clause.	**If** she **gets** married next year, I'll go to the wedding. *(future idea in the if clause, but the verb form is the present)* They are planning to take a trip to Florida before they **get** married. *(not: before they will get married)*

2. *Combine the sentences, using the word(s) in parentheses. Rewrite the sentences.*

    a. They got married. They were sixteen and seventeen. (when)

       They got married when they were sixteen and seventeen.

    b. Jennifer wanted to wait to have children. She finished school. (until)

    c. However, she got pregnant. She finished high school. (before)

    d. She won a scholarship to a university. She had a baby. (three years after)

    e. You don't have an education. It is hard to find a good job. (if)

    f. You have young children. It is hard to study. (when)

    g. She completes her degree. She will be able to get a better job. (after)

    h. Maranda will be happier. The judge makes a final decision. (when)

    i. Maranda moves in with Steven's family. She will miss her mother. (if)

ANSWER KEY

3. *Correct the mistakes in these sentences. Remember to check the punctuation!*

a. If Jennifer ~~will be~~ *is* in class all day, it is hard for her to take care of Maranda.

b. Children need to be with their mothers when they will be young.

c. When Jennifer finishes school she will be able to give Maranda a better life.

d. After Steven will grow up and have more experiences in the world he will be a better husband and father.

e. If Maranda lives with her grandmother, whenever she will miss her mother.

f. If Maranda is in a good day care her mother will not worry.

DECISION NOTE: *Jennifer appealed Judge Cashen's decision. Here is the result. What is your opinion? Discuss with a partner.*

Jennifer Ireland's lawyer appealed Judge Cashen's decision. The higher court said that Judge Cashen was wrong to consider day care in making this decision. The higher court gave custody of Maranda to her mother.

Editing Checklist

Check the Content

1. *Exchange your opinion letter with a classmate's. After you read your classmate's letter, answer the following questions.*

   ❏ Are the opinions clear?
   ❏ Are there enough details?

Check the Details

2. *Reread your letter. If necessary, revise what you wrote. Try to change unclear words or sentences. Add more reasons if necessary. Then continue checking your own letter. Use these questions.*

   ❏ Did you use *should* or *ought to*? A sentence with *if* ? Are the verb forms correct?
   ❏ Did you use transition words to give examples or explain reasons? Check the punctuation with these words.
   ❏ Did you use formal letter format?

3. *Make your corrections. Rewrite your letter.*

Vocabulary Log

What words or phrases would you like to remember from this chapter? Write five to ten items in your notebook. Examples are on page 10.

Grammar and Punctuation Review

Look over your writing from this chapter. What changes did you need to make in grammar and punctuation? Write them in your notebook. Review them before the next writing assignment.

Chapter 21

Discipline

Customs about raising children vary from one group of people to another. In this chapter you will read a poem and an essay about the ways parents discipline children.

Starting Point

Parental Discipline

Most people would agree that children sometimes need to be disciplined. However, people don't always agree on the method of discipline.

1. *Discuss these questions with a partner or a small group.*

    a. Do you remember a time when you were young, when your parents were furious with you?
    b. What made them so angry?
    c. What did they do about it?
    d. How did you feel?

2. *Read the following poem about discipline.*

> **Beat**
> by Janet Wong
>
> When I was small
> they spanked me
> with a newspaper
> rolled tight,
> and I would yell
> until the neighbors
> opened their warped
> wooden windows.
>
> Now they have learned a better way,
> and the pain hurts worse
> than a whipping
> when they shake
> their heads, whispering,
> "We are so ashamed,"
> in a room so quiet
> you hear them
> swallow.

3. *Fill in the chart with words from the poem and your own inferences to complete this comparison of the poet's punishment then and now.*

ANSWER KEY

	Before	*Now*
The way the parents punished		
The level of noise		
The way the writer feels		

4. *Do you understand the feelings of this poet? Did your parents ever make you feel terrible without saying very much? Is this method of discipline effective? Discuss these questions with a partner or a small group.*

5. *Consider the following situations. What would you do if you were the parent? Write your ideas on the lines.*

a. Your teenager has been arguing a lot with you. Today she is being very pleasant.

_____

_____

b. Your teenager was supposed to be home at midnight. He came home at 2 a.m.

_____

_____

c. Your three-year-old is screaming in the grocery store because she wants some candy.

_____

_____

d. Your three-year-old is always hitting other children and taking their toys.

_____

_____

Reading

Teaching Children How to Behave

READING TIP

The main idea of a paragraph or reading is usually the most general idea. **Specific details** support the main idea. When you look for the main idea, decide which ideas are specific and which are more general.

This essay relates changes in the ways parents discipline children.

1. *Read the following selection.*

Teaching Children How to Behave

[1] In the last thirty years, the ways that many parents in the United States discipline their children have changed. In the past, when a child behaved badly, many parents spanked the child on the bottom. Now, however, they usually use less violent forms of punishment. They also focus more on *discipline* and less on *punishment,* and they try to encourage good behavior.

[2] Experts say that parents should model good behavior. For example, if you don't want your child to use a loud voice, use a soft voice yourself. Also, you should focus on the good behavior, not the bad. Children want praise, so parents should tell children when they are doing a good job. Children will continue to do things that parents praise them for. Praise is more effective than complaining about bad behavior is. Rewards also help. Parents can tell children, "If you are quiet in the restaurant, we will have dessert." Then parents have to follow through with any promises of rewards or punishment.

[3] Of course, these methods do not eliminate bad behavior. Children will always test their parents to see how far they can go. What should parents do then? The answer depends on the situation. Young children want their parents' attention, so sometimes leaving the room is effective. Say, "I am going to leave the room until you stop (doing something)." Most parents also use "time out" with young children. During time out, children have to sit by themselves for a certain amount of time.

[4] What should parents do when older children misbehave? Older children usually want to spend a lot of time with their friends, so "grounding" is a very common punishment. When children are grounded, they have to spend their free time at home. They cannot do things with their friends. Taking away games or favorite activities is also a very common form of punishment.

[5] There are still a lot of people who follow the more traditional methods of child discipline and punishment, such as spanking. Some people

think that parents nowadays are not strict enough. However, new theories of childrearing don't say that parents shouldn't be *strict*. They encourage parents to use different methods of enforcing their rules.

In Chapter 19, you found the writer's main ideas. The next exercise helps you analyze how the writer supports the main idea with details.

2. *Are the following statements main ideas or details? Write* **MI** *for "main idea" or* **D** *for "detail" on the line.*

ANSWER KEY

a. __D__ Many parents used to spank children.

b. _____ Many parents now use less violent forms of punishment.

c. _____ Parents focus more on overall discipline than on punishment.

d. _____ Children want praise.

e. _____ Parents should use a soft voice as one model of good behavior.

f. _____ There are ways to encourage good behavior.

g. _____ Dessert may be a reward for good behavior in a restaurant.

h. _____ The type of discipline to use depends on the age of the children.

i. _____ "Grounding" means forcing a child to stay at home.

3. *Write the letter of the correct answer on the line.*

ANSWER KEY

The main idea of this reading is that _____.

a. physical punishment is not effective.
b. today many parents think that discipline does not include punishment.
c. there are different ways to discipline children.

4. *Are these sentences true or false? Write **T** or **F** in the blanks.*

a. _T_ Many people have new ideas about disciplining children.

b. ____ Spanking used to be a common method for parents to punish their children.

c. ____ *Discipline* means teaching children how to behave.

d. ____ Punishment usually follows good behavior.

e. ____ "Time out" works well with older children.

f. ____ *Grounding* means taking away a favorite game.

g. ____ No one spanks their children anymore.

h. ____ Experts say that parents should not be strict with their children.

5. *Consider again the situations in exercise 5 on page 181. According to the reading on page 182–183, what might be a typical parent's response in the United States? Discuss your answers with a partner.*

Quickwriting: The Best Way to Discipline

What do you think is the best way to discipline a young child? A teenager? In your notebook, write for five or ten minutes about these questions.

Vocabulary Log

What words or phrases would you like to remember from this chapter? Write five to ten items in your notebook. Examples are on page 10.

Class Activity — Interview and Report

1. Interview several people of different ages.

2. Ask them what they think is the best way to discipline a young child and a teenager.

3. Make a chart with your interview results.

4. Report back to class.

Chapter 22

That's Life!

Is family life easier or harder for people now than it was fifty years ago? This chapter gives you an opportunity to brainstorm ideas and write your opinion about this question.

Starting Point

Changes

A lot of changes in society have affected relationships and roles in families. Fifty years ago the gender roles were clearer than they are now: Most men worked outside the home and most women were responsible for everything in the home.

Do the parents in your family have different roles than their parents had? How are the roles different? Discuss with a partner or a small group.

Reading

Here's Why Wives Complain

Stereotypes are often unfair generalizations. This selection takes a new look at an old stereotype about men and women.

1. *Read the following selection.*

Here's Why Wives Complain

Here's Why Wives COMPLAIN

It is a common generalization: wives complain and husbands withdraw. A new study helps explain why — and it has little to do with typical gender stereotypes.

Researchers at Ohio State University studied a typical communication problem: "demand-withdraw." In demand-withdraw, one person asks for change. The other either doesn't answer or ignores the request. For example, in a typical scene in many marriages, the wife asks the husband for help.

The husband doesn't answer.

Is gender the reason for the difference in behavior in this situation? Researchers don't think so. They think that women, who are still responsible for most household and child-care jobs, have more to gain from complaining in this situation. Husbands, however, generally withdraw from these conversations. They benefit from keeping things the same — not having to help. They hope that they will not have to change anything. Again, it is not gender that makes men withdraw — it is the situation and how much they will lose by agreeing to change. ◄

2. *Complete these sentences. Find words in the reading with the same meaning as the words in parentheses.*

ANSWER KEY

a. Sometimes you feel better when you _____. If you don't

express your feelings, you may become more unhappy about

things. (express unhappiness)

b. The idea that girls can't play sports is a _____. (generalization)

c. Their _____ wasn't important. Both groups gave the

same answers. (male or female)

d. When the discussion turned into an argument, many people

decided to _____ from the conversation. They didn't

want to argue. (not participate)

e. Women would _____ from the change because they

would get more free time. (gain something)

3. *These are several examples from the reading. What are they examples of? Write the correct letter on the line.*

ANSWER KEY

a. "Wives complain and husbands withdraw."

b. ". . . the wife asks the husband for help."

c. "The husband doesn't answer."

d. "Demand-withdraw"

e. Male or female, husband or wife

_____ a communication problem

_____ gender

_____ demand

_____ withdraw

_____ a stereotype

4. *Find words that are related in each list. Words may be related in several ways. Cross out the word that does **not** belong in each list.*

a. researchers	~~gain~~	study	explain
b. (be) responsible (for)	child care	communication	help
c. ignore	gender	ask	complain
d. ask	household	agree	demand
e. ignore	gain	benefit	lose
f. husbands	marriages	wives	answer
g. gender	household	male	female

5. *Complete the paragraph below with words from exercise 4. You may use the same word more than once.*

a. In traditional _*marriages*_ , women are _____

for _____ and most household jobs. When women

ask men for _____ , men often _____

their request.

b. _____ at Ohio State University decided to study

a typical problem in marriages: the way that _____

and _____ communicate. The researchers'

_____ found that differences in the way men and

women communicated were related to how much they had

to gain or lose in the discussion. _____ was not

the main reason for the differences.

c. Wives have more to _____ when they

_____ about how much work they have. Men

have more to _____, so they often try to

_____ the demand.

d. Although the _____ studied communication in

_____, this study probably relates to many differ-

ent situations where one person has more to _____

from change than another does.

....

Writing

Family life changes with each generation. These brainstorming activities will help you discuss your opinion about some of these changes.

Preparing to Write: Brainstorming

1. *Complete this survey. Put a check (✓) by your opinions.*

a. For men, life is _____ ☐ easier ☐ harder ☐ the same
today ~~than~~ than it   than   than   as
was fifty years ago.

b. For women, life is _____ ☐ easier ☐ harder ☐ the same
today ~~than~~ than it   than   than   as
was fifty years ago.

c. For teenagers, life is _____ ☐ easier ☐ harder ☐ the same
today ~~than~~ than it   than   than   as
was fifty years ago.

2. *Work with a group of your classmates. Discuss your opinions. Make a large chart like this one, and write your opinions in it. Then share your ideas with the rest of the class.*

	easier because (list reasons)	**harder because** (list reasons)
For men, life is		
For women, life is		
For teenagers, life is		

Writing an Opinion

Now it's time to write your opinion about changes in family life.

Choose one of these groups: men, women, or teenagers. Write about your ideas. You might begin with a sentence like "For men, life is . . . than it was fifty years ago."

Writers often make comparisons to show differences and similarities.

1. *Read these guidelines for writing comparisons.*

Rules	Examples
The **comparative** form is used to compare two things. Don't forget to include **than** when you mention both.	Life is **easier** now **than** before. Family life is **more difficult than** it used to be.
Use **as . . . as** to show similarity or lack of similarity.	Women work **as** hard **as** men. Their salaries are not **as** high (**as** men's salaries).
The **superlative** is used to talk about one thing in comparison to more than one other thing. Don't forget to use *the* before *most.*	This is **the easiest** exercise in the book. The teenage years are **the most difficult** (of all the years).

See page 197 in Reference for a list of **comparative and superlative forms**.

2. *Put a check (✓) in front of the correct sentence(s).*

a. _____ This is the easier exercise in this book.

b. _____ This exercise is easier than the last one.

c. _____ Parents need to give teenagers as much freedom than they can.

d. _____ The most difficult task is editing my own work.

e. _____ Reading a paragraph is easier reading poetry.

f. _____ Many reading tasks are difficult, but reading a news-paper is most difficult.

3. *Correct the errors in these sentences.*

                better

a. His work is much ~~good~~ than before.

b. It's easier for me to write paragraphs to write poetry.

c. Swimming is best exercise for your back.

d. I think poetry is difficult to understand than other kinds of writing.

e. Telephoning is expensive than faxing.

f. I think this is best job anyone could have.

g. It is as hard for women now than it was twenty years ago.

h. Is it more kinder to tell the truth or to lie in this situation?

i. We tried harder this time before.

j. It's most difficult thing I have ever tried to do.

Editing Checklist

Check the Content

1. *Exchange your opinion with a classmate. After you read what your classmate wrote, answer these questions.*

   ❑ Did the writer state his or her opinion clearly?
   ❑ Are there enough details?

Check the Details

2. *Reread your opinion. If necessary, revise what you wrote. Add more reasons or examples. Then continue checking your own writing. Use these questions.*

   ❑ Check the forms of the comparatives and superlatives. Did you include *than* and *the* when necessary?
   ❑ Did you use words to give examples or explain reasons? Check the punctuation with these words.
   ❑ Check each verb. Is the form correct? The tense?

3. *Make your corrections. Rewrite your opinion on a separate piece of paper.*

Vocabulary Log

What words or phrases would you like to remember from this chapter? Write five to ten items in your notebook. Examples are on page 10.

Grammar and Punctuation Review

Look over your writing from this chapter. What changes did you need to make in grammar and punctuation? Write them in your notebook.

Review all the grammar and punctuation problems you recorded in your notebook. Make a list of the ones that you still need to work on.

Reference

BUSINESS LETTER FORMAT

The format of a business letter is more formal than a personal letter.

This example is the **full block style.** All the lines of text are lined up on the left.

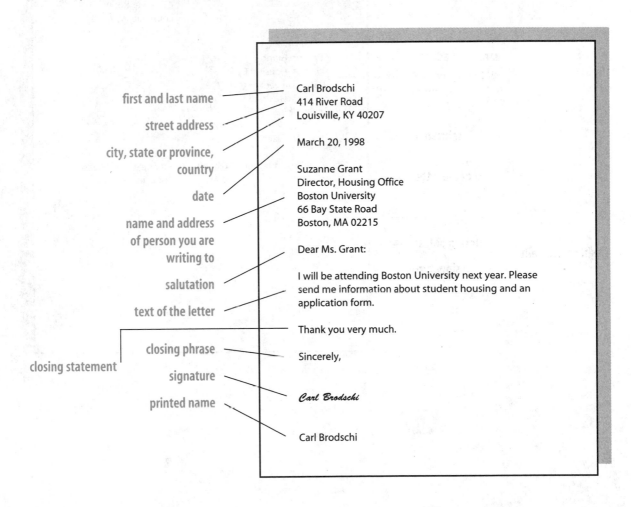

first and last name — Carl Brodschi
street address — 414 River Road
city, state or province, country — Louisville, KY 40207

date — March 20, 1998

name and address of person you are writing to —
Suzanne Grant
Director, Housing Office
Boston University
66 Bay State Road
Boston, MA 02215

salutation — Dear Ms. Grant:

text of the letter —
I will be attending Boston University next year. Please send me information about student housing and an application form.

Thank you very much.

closing statement — closing phrase — Sincerely,

signature —

printed name — *Carl Brodschi*

Carl Brodschi

This is the **modified block style.** The first line of each paragraph may be indented three spaces.

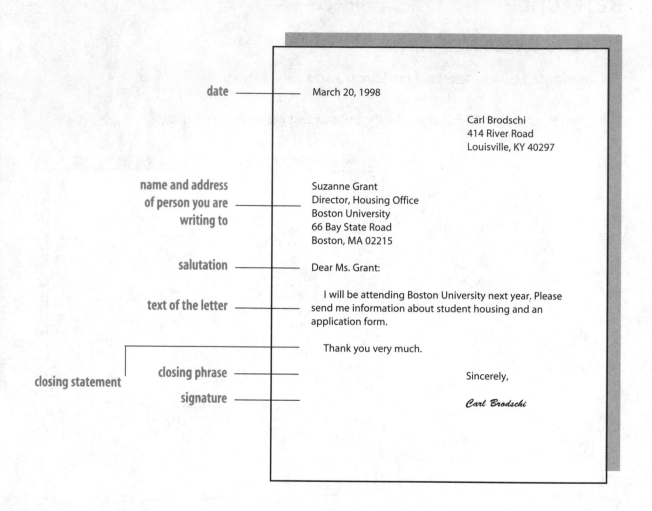

date — March 20, 1998

Carl Brodschi
414 River Road
Louisville, KY 40297

name and address
of person you are — Suzanne Grant
writing to Director, Housing Office
Boston University
66 Bay State Road
Boston, MA 02215

salutation — Dear Ms. Grant:

text of the letter — I will be attending Boston University next year. Please send me information about student housing and an application form.

Thank you very much.

closing statement

closing phrase — Sincerely,

signature — Carl Brodschi

COMPARATIVES AND SUPERLATIVES

Use these rules to form the comparative and superlative forms of adjectives, adverbs, and nouns.

Rule	Comparative	Superlative	Example
one-syllable adjective or adverb	-er . . . than	the . . . -est	**faster** than (fast) the **hardest** (hard)
two-syllable adjective or adverb ending in **-y;** change the **y** to **i**	-ier . . . than	the . . . -iest	**easier** than (easy) the **busiest** (busy)
adjective or adverb of two (or more) syllables	more . . . than	the most . . .	more **exciting** the most **enthusiastic**
count noun	more . . . than fewer . . . than	the most . . . the fewest . . .	more **jobs** than the most **jobs** fewer **rewards** than the fewest **rewards**
non-count noun	more . . . than less . . . than	the most . . . the least . . .	more **discipline** than the most **discipline** less **money** than the least **money**
irregular forms	**good** **well** **bad** **badly** **far**	**better** **better** **worse** **worse** **farther**	**the best** **the best** **the worst** **the worst** **the farthest**

SPELLING RULES FOR ADDING ENDINGS

To apply spelling rules, remember that the vowels in English are *a, e, i, o,* and *u.* The rest of the letters are consonants. When you add endings to nouns or verbs, follow these rules:

Plural Noun Endings

For most nouns	add *-s.*	book	books
For nouns that end in *s, x, ch,* or *sh*	add *-es.*	box wish	boxes wishes
For nouns that end in *z*	double the *z* and add *-es.*	quiz	quizzes
For nouns that end in a consonant + *y*	change the *y* to *i* and add *-es.*	delivery	deliveries

Verb Endings

For verbs that end in a consonant + *e*	drop the *-e* and add *-ing* or *-ed.*	hope	hoping	hoped
For one-syllable verbs that end in one vowel + a consonant	double the consonant and add *-ing* or *-ed.*	stop	stopping	stopped
For two-syllable verbs that have the stress on the second syllable and end in a vowel + a consonant	double the consonant and add *-ing* or *-ed.*	omit	omitting	omitted
For verbs that end in a consonant + *y*	change the *y* to *i* and add *-ed* or *-es.*	try	tried	tries
For verbs that end in *o, (t)ch, s, sh, x,* or *z*	add *-es.*	do match toss wish fix buzz	does matches tosses wishes fixes buzzes	

IRREGULAR SIMPLE PAST TENSE VERBS

Base	Simple Past	Past Participle	Base	Simple Past	Past Participle
awake	awoke	awoken	fall	fell	fallen
bear	born	born	feed	fed	fed
beat	beat	beaten	feel	felt	felt
become	became	become	fight	fought	fought
begin	began	begun	find	found	found
bend	bent	bent	fit	fit	fit
bet	bet	bet	fly	flew	flown
bid	bid	bid	forbid	forbid/forbade	forbidden
bite	bit	bitten	forget	forgot	forgotten
bleed	bled	bled	forgive	forgave	forgiven
blow	blew	blown	freeze	froze	frozen
break	broke	broken	get	got	gotten
bring	brought	brought			(*British:* got)
build	built	built	give	gave	given
burn	burnt/burned	burnt/burned	go	went	gone
burst	burst	burst	grind	ground	ground
buy	bought	bought	grow	grew	grown
cast	cast	cast	hang	hung	hung
catch	caught	caught	have	had	had
choose	chose	chosen	hear	heard	heard
come	came	come	hide	hid	hidden/hid
cost	cost	cost	hit	hit	hit
creep	crept	crept	hold	held	held
cut	cut	cut	hurt	hurt	hurt
deal	dealt	dealt	keep	kept	kept
dig	dug	dug	knit	knit	knitted
dive	dove	dived	know	knew	known
	(*British:* dived)		lay	laid	laid
do	did	done	lead	led	led
draw	drew	drawn	leave	left	left
dream	dreamt/dreamed	dreamt/dreamed	lend	lend	lend
drink	drank	drunk	let	let	let
drive	drove	driven	lie	lay	lain
eat	ate	eaten	light	lit/lighted	lit/lighted
make	made	made	lost	lost	lost
mean	meant	meant	slit	slit	slit
make	made	made	speak	sloke	spoken
meet	met	met	spend	spent	spent
put	put	put	spin	spun	spun
prove	proved	proved/proven	split	split	split
quit	quit	quit	spread	spread	spread
read	read	read	spring	sprang	sprung
rid	rid	rid	stand	stood	stood
ride	rode	ridden	steal	stole	stolen
ring	rang	rung	stick	stuck	stuck
rise	rose	risen	sting	stung	stung
run	ran	run	strike	struck	struck
say	said	said	swear	swore	sworn
see	saw	seen	sweep	swept	swept
seek	sought	sought	swim	swam	swum
sell	sold	sold	swing	swung	swung
send	sent	sent	take	took	taken
set	set	set	teach	taught	taught
shake	shook	shaken	tear	tore	torn
shine	shone	shone	tell	told	told
shoot	shot	shot	think	thought	thought
shrink	shrank	shrunk	throw	threw	thrown
shut	shut	shut	wake	woke	woken
sing	sang	sung	wear	wore	worn
sink	sank	sunk	wet	wet	wet
sit	sat	sat	win	won	won
sleep	slept	slept	withdraw	withdrew	withdrawn
slide	slid	slid	wind	wound	wound or winded

NONCOUNT NOUNS

Some nouns do not have a plural form because we cannot count them. We call these *noncount* nouns. Follow these rules when you use a noncount noun:

Rules	Examples
Noncount nouns are singular. If they are the subject of the sentence, the verb must be singular too.	The **milk is** on the table. His **news is** not good. The **homework was** easy.
Do not use *a* or *an* with a noncount noun.	We need **milk.**
Use a quantity expression to make a noncount noun countable.	Please get **a gallon of milk.** I have **lots of homework** tonight.

Here are some common noncount nouns:

Groups of similar items	art, clothing, equipment, food, fruit, furniture, garbage, grammar, homework, information, luggage, mail, money, music, news, research, slang, traffic, vocabulary, work
Liquids	beer, blood, coffee, cream, gasoline, honey, juice, milk, oil, shampoo, soda, soup, tea, water, wine
Things that can be cut into smaller pieces	bread, butter, cheese, cotton, film, glass, gold, ice, iron, meat, paper, silver, wood
Things that have very small parts	dirt, flour, grass, hair, rice, sand, sugar
Gases	air, fog, pollution, smog, smoke, steam
Ideas that you cannot touch	advice, anger, beauty, communication, education, fun, happiness, health, help, love, luck, peace, sleep, space, time, truth, wealth
Fields of study	business administration, engineering, nursing
Activities	soccer, swimming, tennis, traveling
Diseases and illnesses	cancer, cholera, flu, heart disease, malaria, polio, smallpox, strep throat
Facts or events of nature	darkness, electricity, fire, fog, heat, light, lightning, rain, snow, sunshine, thunder, weather, wind
Languages	Arabic, Chinese, Turkish, Russian

TRANSITION EXPRESSIONS

When you combine sentences or ideas, transition expressions help make your ideas clear.

Start with two separate ideas or sentences.	I ate breakfast. I went to the store at 10:00 a.m.
Combine the ideas with a **preposition.**	I went to the store **after** breakfast.
Combine the ideas with a **subordinate conjunction.**	I went to the store **after** I ate breakfast. I ate breakfast **before** I went to the store.
Combine the ideas with an **adverbial expression.**	I ate breakfast. **After that,** I went to the store. I went to the store. **Before that,** I ate breakfast.

Here are some common transition expressions.

Prepositions	Subordinate Conjunctions	Adverbial Expressions
Time in a Sequence		
after, before, until • We waited **until** 3:15.	**after, before, until (till)** • We waited **until** they **first.**	**at this point, before that, in the past, (not) long ago, after that, at first, in the future** (*to express time before the present*) • We weren't angry **at** came. • **At first,** we weren't angry.
Listing		
		first, in the first place, in the second place, later on, then, after that, next, finally, last • **First,** try to write down the problem. **Then,** telephone the landlord.
At the Same Time		
during • They watch TV **during** dinner.	**when, as, while, as long as** • They watch TV **when** they eat dinner.	**meanwhile, at the same time, at that time** • I waited in line at the ticket counter. **Meanwhile,** my father returned the rental car.

Prepositions	Subordinate Conjunctions	Adverbial Expressions
Contrast		
unlike, in contrast to	**but, while,**	**however, in contrast, on the other hand**
• **Unlike** my sister, I like cold weather.	• I like cold weather, **but** my sister doesn't.	• I like cold weather. My sister, **on the other hand,** hates it.
Cause-Effect, Results, Reasons		
because of, as a result of,	**because, since, so, as,**	**for this reason, because of this, as a result, therefore, so**
• She was unhappy **because of** her living situation.	• She was unhappy **because** she didn't like her roommates. • Her roommates never talked to her, **so** she didn't feel comfortable in her apartment.	• Her roommates almost never spoke. **Because of this,** she was very unhappy in her apartment.
Condition		
	if, unless,	
	• **If** it rains, we won't go to the beach. • We'll go to the beach **unless** it rains.	
Examples		
such as		**for example**
• I like sports **such as** ice skating that keep you warm in the winter.		• Some winter sports are better than others. **For example,** ice-skating keeps you warm and is great exercise.

Answer Key

I First Things First

CHAPTER 1

Targeting: Country, Language, and Nationality Words (*pages 6–8*)

2. (*page 6*)

Mexico	Mexican	Spanish
answers will vary	answers will vary	Spanish
Kuwait	Kuwaiti	Arabic
Canada	Canadian	English/French
Korea	Korean	Korean
Germany	German	German
Japan	Japanese	Japanese

Answers in last two rows will vary.

3. (*page 7*)

a. 2. Arabic; 3. French; 4. Germany

b. 5. (any South American country); 6. Japanese; 7. Korea

c. 8. Mexican; 9. Mexico

d. 10. Chinese

4. (*page 8*)

b. Brazil; c. Colombia; d. Japanese; e. Indian; f. Greek; g. America; h. Arabic

CHAPTER 2

Starting Point (*pages 12–13*)

2. (*page 13*)

Answers may vary. Possible answers include the following:

a. student . . . he is young and carrying a backpack; b. musician; c. ice skater . . . she is carrying ice skates; d. business person . . . she is carrying a briefcase.

Reading (*pages 14–15*)

2. (*page 15*)

a. math and science teacher; b. a volunteer in the Big Brother Program; c. a figure skating champion *or* an ice-skating champion; d. a bank robber

Targeting: Adjectives and Nouns (*pages 15–16*)

2. (*page 16*)

adjectives: a, c, d, e, i, k, l
nouns: b, f, g, h, j

Editing and Rewriting (*pages 18–19*)

2. (*page 18*)

Correct sentences are b, c, and e.

3. (*page 19*)

Khalid Al-Shafi is from Kuwait. He is studying English at Boston University. He lives in a dormitory at the university on Commonwealth Avenue. His roommate's name is Peter Jones. Peter and Khalid get along very well. They have only one problem. Peter likes to get up early. Khalid, on the other hand, never goes to bed before 1:00 a.m. This is a big problem for both students. They are thinking about changing roommates.

CHAPTER 3

Reading (*pages 22–24*)

2. (*pages 22–23*)

a. 425 dollars per/a month; bedroom *or* bedrooms

b. His apartment is too crowded. He needs a quiet place to study.

c. *Answers will vary.* (opinion)

d. He can study at school.

e. *Answers will vary.* (opinion)

3. (*pages 23–24*)

a. Van Ly should try to work with what he has.

b. He should try to work this out with his family first, and then think about moving out on his own.

Targeting: Collocations (*pages 24–25*)

2. (*page 25*)

a. cost to; b. afford to; c. make; d. cost; e. spend . . . on/for; f. afford; g. costs . . . for; h. on

Preparing to Write 2: Introductory Sentences (*pages 26–27*)

1. (*pages 26–27*)

a. Sometimes young people and parents have different ideas about when the young people will move away from home.

b. Married couples usually want to live on their own.

c. It costs a lot to live on your own.

d. It is important for young people to experience living on their own.

2 Where in the World?

CHAPTER 4

Reading (*pages 31–32*)

2. (*pages 32–33*)

faraway

soft adventure travel: fishing (*given*), hiking, bird watching, trail riding; *hard adventure travel:* white-water rafting (*given,*) mountain climbing

reasons:
. . . nature and the outdoors cities;
. . . exciting, new experiences with the help of experienced guides
communities are
3. (*page 32*)
hard adventure travel: mountain climbing, river rafting; *soft adventure travel:* city tour, park, bus tour through the Rockies

Targeting: Adjectives to Describe Places (*pages 34–35*)

1. (*page 34*)
b, g, d, f, c, a, e

CHAPTER 5

Starting Point (*pages 36–37*)

3. (*page 37*)
b. daily; c. single; d. includes; e. shared; f. double; g. cost; h. spend; i. planning

Reading 1 (*pages 38–39*)

1. each person; 2. $630; 3. regular season; 4. peak season; 5. $134; 6. $144; 7. $800; 8. yes

Reading 2 (*pages 39–41*)

2. (*page 40*)
b. ways; c. strangers; d. transportation; e. trailer; f. deposit; g. advance; h. round-trip; i. deliver; j. discount; k. reservations
3. (*page 41*)
hitchhiking: don't always get a ride; it's dangerous riding with strangers; *transportation company:* have to pay for gas and make a deposit; have to find a way back home; *courier:* no advance planning possible; *discount fares:* must purchase ticket two to three weeks in advance; must travel in middle of the week; must buy round-trip ticket

Targeting: Nouns and Verbs (*pages 42–43*)

2. (*pages 42–43*)
nouns: b, c, e, h, j, k, n; *verbs:* a (*given*), d, f, g, i, l, m
3. (*page 43*)
an: a, c, e, f, j; *a:* b, g, h, i, k no article necessary: d, l

Preparing to Write (*page 44*)

2. Please send me; 3. I'd like to; 4. What; 5. Please tell me; 6. How; 7. Where; 8. I'd like to; 9. Do

CHAPTER 6

Starting Point (*page 47*)

2. (*page 47*)
b. b; c. a; d. b; e. b; f. b

Reading (*pages 48–49*)

2. (*page 49*)
b. develop; c. prize; d. flight; e. challenges; f. spacecraft; g. affordable; h. reusable; I. safe; j. destination; k. light years; l. first-class; m. atmosphere; n. unique
3. (*page 49*)
a. yes; b. (part 1) affordable, reusable, safe, (part 2) safe; c. No—just 60 miles into space; d. no; e. *Answers will vary.*

Targeting: Adjectives to Describe an Experience, (*pages 50–54*)

2. (*page 51*)
Positive: incredible, interesting, nice, exciting, relaxing, wonderful, spectacular
Negative: boring, depressing, tiring, uncomfortable
Neutral: typical
Positive or negative: challenging, cold, hot

Preparing to Write (*pages 52*)

2. (*page 53*)
b. Mrs. Tom Jones, . . . Street; c. Dallas, Texas; d. Company . . . South; e. 110 West Broadway; f. Lois Laney; g. Jane Goodman; h. Hill; i. Mrs. . . . CA (same line) 92117; j. Spring Street. . . . (new line) Menlo Park, CA 96025
3. (*pages 53–54*)
a. Mark Hammond
   9500 25th Avenue or Ave.
   Columbus, Ohio 43202
b. Rita Hernandez
   Director of Marketing
   Crane Company
   4200 NW 107th Ave. or Avenue
   Miami, Florida 33172

Editing and Rewriting (*pages 55–56*)

2. (*page 56*)
correct: a, c, e
3. (*page 56*)
b. The train almost always leaves on time.
d. The bus tour of the mountain usually takes four hours.
f. We are staying with friends for now.
g. The travel guide usually says "Don't worry" just before we have a big problem.

3 Living Spaces

CHAPTER 8

Reading (*pages 66–67*)

1. (*pages 66–67*)
c, d, a, b

3. (*page 67*)
ceiling, furniture, chairs, walls, tables, rug, *kotatsu* or foot warmer, floor, heater, blanket, chest, bookcase, couches, pillows, television set, bookshelves, books, pictures, electronic equipment, piano, windows, decorations

Targeting: Spatial Prepositions (*pages 68–69*)
Answers to some items may vary. Possible answers are:
2. along; 3. with; 4. under; 5. facing; 6. On; 7. next to; 8. with; 9. above; 10. under

Preparing to Write (*pages 69–70*)
1. (*pages 69–70*)
a. the second description; b. the first description

Editing and Rewriting (*pages 71–73*)
2. (*page 71*)
correct: b, e
3. (*page 72*)
correct: b, c
4. (*pages 72–73*)
a. are; b. is; c. are; d. is; e. are; f. is; g. do; h. has; i. have; j. There is; k. wash; l. rinse; m. get; n. are; o. take; p. is; q. are; r. goes; s. misses
5. (*page 73*)
a. correct; b. . . . table, a rug, . . .; c. jacks, a cable TV hook-up, . . .; d. . . . painting, two photographs, . . . e. . . .; TV, a video, . . .; f. correct; g. correct

CHAPTER 9

Starting Point (*pages 76–77*)
1. (*pages 76–77*)
(top to bottom:) Swiss, Southeast Asian, Balinese (*given*), Mediterranean, North American

Reading (*pages 78–81*)
2. (*pages 79–80*)
a. Southern Europe, also South Pacific; b. patio covered by grape vines *or cardak*; c. Buddhist homes, small area set up to remember gods and ancestors; d. Korea, China, parts of Latin America, houses built around courtyards and rooms that open onto common outdoor space; e. Japan, place for footwear in front entrance; f. cold areas of the United States and Canada, "mud rooms" where people leave boots and heavy coats; g. some Muslim countries, separate areas for males and females
3. (*page 81*)
a. *cleanliness:* mud room, cold areas of the United States and Canada, place for shoes in Japan; *privacy:*

separate male and female areas in Muslim countries; *formality:* family room separate
b. *religious custom:* separate male and female areas in the United States, in homes in some Muslim countries, in many Buddhist homes, small area set up to remember gods or ancestors
c. *Answers will vary.*

CHAPTER 10

Reading (*pages 86–88*)
1. (*pages 88–89*)
2. a. consider; b. benefit; c. crowded; d. lockers; e. belongings; f. fund; g. covered
3. (*page 89*)
a. study *or* rest; b. the college president; c. a different; d. *Answers will vary.* (opinion)
4. (*pages 89–90*)
a. *time*—A, B; *cafeteria*—A, B; *library*—B; *personal*—A, B
b. a smoking area, a coffee shop, a computer lab
c. *their reasons*—A; *their ideas*—B

CHAPTER 11

Starting Point (*pages 91–92*)
1. d. (*page 92*)
there is a leak in the top story apartment; there is a broken window; a carpet is old and worn-out; the light is broken in the hallway; the elevator doesn't work; the furnace doesn't work; there are cockroaches in a kitchen; the yard is a mess; all the apartments need new paint.

Reading (*pages 93–95*)
2. (*page 94*)
j, d, e, h, k, a, b, f, i, g, c
5. (*pages 94–95*)
1. speak to your landlord; 2. write to your landlord by certified mail; 3. keep copies of your correspondence or a record of your conversations; 4. see if there is a housing commission in your area—if there is, file a complaint with it; 5. talk to a lawyer; 6. stop paying your rent; 7. make repairs and deduct the cost from your rent

Targeting: Word Forms (*pages 95–96*)
1. (*page 95*)
make a complaint, owner, building, respond (to), deduct
2. (*page 96*)
a. respond; b. building; c. deduct; d. owner; e. payment; f. complaint

4 The E-mail Revolution

CHAPTER 12

Starting Point (*pages 101–102*)

2. e-mail messages; 3. communications software; 4. modem; 5. the Internet

Reading (*pages 102–104*)

2. (*page 103*)
b, d, c, e, a (*given*)
3. (*page 103*)
b. It's cheaper than regular mail c. It's very convenient. d. You can print messages and save them. e. It's good for the environment. f. It's your doorway to the Internet. (*also possible:* Everyone is equal on e-mail *or* It is a world without time zones or borders.)
4. (*page 104*)
a. meet; b. talk; c. snail mail; d. superhighway

CHAPTER 13

Starting Point (*pages 105–106*)

2. (*page 106*)
a. F; b. T; c. F; d. F; e. F

Reading (*pages 106–111*)

1. (*pages 106–108*)
B. Studying in Canada; C. Montreal; D. Living in Vancouver; E. Cold and Warm Places
3. (*page 109*)
Message B. 1; Message C. 3; Message D. 2; Message E. 4
4. (*pages 110–111*)
A. alt.auto.toyota; B. alt.sci.communications; C. alt.business.import-export; D. croatia.newsgroup. discussion

Targeting: E-mail Addresses (*pages 111–113*)

1. (*page 112*)
slacey: a, g; gborg: b, f; thiller: c, d; phowell: e, h
3. (*pages 112–113*)
a. .edu; b. .com; c. .org; d. .gov
4. (*page 113*)
a. .ca; b. .tw; c. .uk; d. .ja; e. .mx; f. .se

CHAPTER 14

Starting Point (*page 116*)

1. b; 2. a (*given*); 3. d; 4. g; 5. f; 6. e; 7. c

Reading 1 (*pages 117–121*)

3. (*page 120*)
b. Taiwan; c. a psychiatrist; d. so that people can write their opinions; e. probably not; f. on a mountain • Dave hurt his leg. g. managing e-mail messages; h. He wants to study, but he does not have a lot of money.
4. (*page 121*)
to write to a famous person; to set up an appointment with a doctor; to give your opinion to a politician; to send a private message; to send a message to a friend from anywhere in the world; to communicate at the office; to request information

Reading 2 (*pages 121–124*)

2. (*pages 122–123*)
a. busy, now, fast, won't wait, overnight, 10:30 a.m. the next day, speed; b. fast or rushed
3. (*page 123*)
Wording of answers may vary. a. enjoy getting letters; b. don't write by hand anymore; c. depends on, uses
4. (*page 124*)
a. F; b. T; c. T; d. T; e. T; f. F; g. F

Preparing to Write (*pages 124–125*)

1. (*page 124*) your doctor, your boss, your teacher, your employees, a person you don't know
3. (*page 125*)
a, b, f, g, h

Editing and Rewriting (*pages 126–127*)

1. (*page 126*)
It doesn't say what programs she is interested in. There is also no address or fax number to respond to if you send something by regular mail or fax.
2. (*pages 126–127*)
Dr. Rimple does not give a time for the appointment.

CHAPTER 15

Reading (*pages 130*)

2. Yes.
3. (page 130)
a. employees; b. managers; c. fired; d. inappropriate *or* unprofessional
4. (page 131) b.

Targeting: Expressions for Business Writing

1. (pages 131) column B: e, a (*given*), c, b, f, d
2. (page 132)
a. We would appreciate; b. We have instituted a new policy; c. As you all know, d. As we use personal e-mail more,; e. If you have any questions,; f. We hope that

Editing and Rewriting (pages 133–134)

2. (page 134)
a, c, e
3. (page 134)

a. computers; b. cooperation; c. mail is; d. time; e. many; f. software; g. information; h. e-mail; i. messages

5 A Fish Out of Water

CHAPTER 16

Reading (*pages 138–142*)

2. (*page 138*)
d
3. (*page 139*)
a. 4; b. 2; c. 1; d. 3
4. (*page 140*)
b. home stage; c. honeymoon stage; d. hostility stage; e. humor stage

Targeting: Words to Describe Emotions (*page 142*)

+: happy, excited, interesting, optimistic, interested, wonderful, comfortable, friendly
−: upset, homesick, angry, frustrated, bored, uncomfortable, isolated, awkward, terrible, alone, self-conscious
+/−: challenged

CHAPTER 17

Starting Point (*pages 143–144*)

3. (page 144)
h (given), f, b, c, e, g, i, d, a

Reading (*pages 144–147*)

2. (pages 146)
(Phrases may vary.)
around Evansburg: different, depressing, rural life, bored, homesick, college, quietly, small town, beautiful campus, friendly, people I know, safe; around San Francisco: city, people on the streets, activity, traffic, lock my car
3. (*pages 116–147*)
a. 2; b. 3; c. 2

Editing and Rewriting (*pages 149-150*)

2. (*page 149*)
a, b
3. (*page 149–150*)
b. it is; c. are; d. It is; e. is; f. He; g. am; h. I

CHAPTER 18

Reading (*pages 152–154*)

2. (*page 152*)
b. F; c. T; d. T; e. F; f. T
3. (*page 154*)

a. 1; b. 2. c. 1; d. 2. e. 1; f. 1

Preparing to Write (*pages 154–155*)

2. (*page 155*)
(*Answers may vary.*) You ought to remember you have lived through bad times before.
It's a good idea to volunteer to speak at schools about your experience.
If I were you, I'd look for other people who have lived abroad.
It's a bad idea to stay at home and feel depressed.

Editing and Rewriting (*pages 156–157*)

2. (*page 157*)
b. When I speak to native speaker**s**, it is difficult to understand **them** (pl. signal)
c. (correct)
d. He made **several** (pl. signal) <u>change**s**</u> in his pronunciation, and people understood him better.
e. She had **many** (pl. signal) unpleasant <u>experience**s**</u> on her trip.
f. I called my <u>friend**s**</u> and talked to **them** (pl. signal) about my new life in Chicago.
g. San Diego and San Francisco **are both** (pl. signals) very wonderful <u>cit**ies.**</u>
h. I try to find a **number** (pl. signal) of <u>way**s**</u> to practice my English.
i. I remember **so many** (pl. signal) <u>time**s**</u> I dreamed of coming to this country.
j. <u>Custom**s are**</u> (pl. signal) hard to adjust to.

6 Issues in Family Life

CHAPTER 19

Reading (*pages 160–162*)

2. (*page 161*) b
3. (*page 161*)
a. T; b. F; c. T; d. F; e. T; f. T
4. (*page 162*)
b. both; c. surprise; d. pregnant; e. negative; f. kind; g. patience; h. problem; i. almost; j. perfect; k. downside; l. labels; m. complaining

Editing and Rewriting (*pages 164–167*)

2. (*page 165*)
b, d, e, g
3. (*page 166*)
b. so; c. such as; d. so; e. For example; f. Because; g. so; h. such as; i. Therefore
4. (*page 166–167*)
b. They were tired so they stayed home. *or* Because they were tired, they stayed home.

c. They decided to save money for their daughter's education. Therefore, they stopped going out to eat every day.
d. They used to eat out a lot, so they saved a lot of money when they stopped going out to eat.
e. They wanted to send their children to college, so they needed to save money.
f. Because they wanted to send them to private school, they had to save a lot of money.

CHAPTER 20
Reading (*pages 171–173*)
2. (*page 172*)
Jennifer . . . Maranda's mother; Steven's mother takes
3. (*page 172–173*)
a. got married; b. get divorced; c. lived with; d. got a scholarship; e. day care center; f. got help from; g. have/get custody; h. homemaker . . . take care of

Editing and Rewriting (*pages 175–178*)
2. (*page 177*)
b. . . . until she finished school.; c. . . . before she finished high school.; d. Three years after she had a baby, . . . ; e. If you don't have an education, . . . ; f. It is hard to study when . . . *or* When you have young children, . . . ; g. After she completes her degree, ...*or* She will get a better job after she completes her degree. h. . . . when the judge makes a final decision. *or* When the judge makes a final decision, . . . ; i. If Maranda moves in with Steven's family, . . .
3. (*page 178*)
b. ~~will be~~ are; c. school, ; d. ~~will grow up~~ grows up . . . and ~~have~~ has . . . world, e. ~~whenever~~; f. ~~day~~ care

CHAPTER 21
Starting Point (*pages 180–181*)
3. (*page 181*)
Before: spanked; yell; bad
Now: shake their heads, whispering; quiet; worse

Reading (*pages 182–184*)
2. (*page 183*)
b. MI; c. MI; d. D; e. D; f. MI; g. D; h. MI; i. D
3. (*page 183*)
b
4. (*pages 184*)
b. T; c. T; d. F; e. F; f. F; g. F; h. F

CHAPTER 22
Reading (*pages 186–189*)
2. (*page 187*)
a. complain; b. stereotype; c. gender; d. withdraw; e. benefit
3. (*page 187*)
d, e, b, c, a
4. (*page 188*)
words that do not belong: b. communication; c. gender; d. household; e. ignore; f. answer; g. household
5. (*pages 188–189*)
a. responsible, child care, help, ignore; b. Researchers, husbands-men, wives-women, study, Gender; c. gain, complain, lose, ignore; d. researchers, marriages(s), gain

Editing and Rewriting (*pages 191–192*)
2. (*page 191*)
b, d
3. (*page 192*)
b. It's easier for me to write paragraphs <u>than</u> to write poetry.
c. Swimming is <u>the</u> best exercise for your back.
d. I think poetry is <u>more</u> difficult to understand than other kinds of writing.
e. Telephoning is <u>more</u> expensive than faxing.
f. I think this is <u>the</u> best job anyone could have.
g. It is as hard for women now <u>as</u> it was twenty years ago.
h. Is it <u>kinder</u> to tell the truth or to lie in this situation?
I. We tried harder this time <u>than</u> before.
j. It's <u>the</u> most difficult thing I have ever tried to do.